I0113560

R. Wilkin

Hand-Book in Bee-Culture

R. Wilkin

Hand-Book in Bee-Culture

ISBN/EAN: 9783337311117

Printed in Europe, USA, Canada, Australia, Japan

Cover: Foto ©Andreas Hilbeck / pixelio.de

More available books at **www.hansebooks.com**

HAND-BOOK

IN

BEE-CULTURE

By R. WILKIN, Apiarian,
CADIZ, OHIO.

"So works the busy Bee,
Creatures that, by a rule in nature, teach
The art of order to a peopled kingdom."

PITTSBURGH:
PRINTED BY W. S. HAVEN, CORNER OF WOOD AND THIRD STREETS.
1868.

INTRODUCTION.

As the printing press has had the desirable effect of exterminating witches, fairies, and ghosts, so is it fast exterminating the idea of luck, and substituting in its stead the intelligible and true idea that every effect is produced by some cause.

Who has not considered Bee-Culture a business of chance? and the philosophy of Bees a mere speculation? But a revolution in this pursuit is going on. General intelligence has increased rapidly of late.

There was a time when bees prospered under the most rude management, but the condition of things pertaining to bees has so changed that no one need expect to be permanently successful in their culture, except he understands the whys and wherefores of the various phenomena of bees, so as to adapt himself to them.

The following articles are only a synopsis of the subject, and to one wishing full instructions they will, in many particulars, not be satisfying. To all such I would recommend "Mysteries of Bee-keeping," by M. Quinby, St. Johnsville, New York; or "The Honey Bee," by L. L. Langstroth, Oxford, Ohio. Both these works are very valuable and interesting. Whoever keeps five hives of bees, with the information such books afford, will likely derive more profit from them than he will with twice the number without that knowledge.

The American Bee Journal, published by S. Wagoner, of Washington, D. C., will keep one posted in what is doing in the business. Knowledge will not move all obstacles out of the way. It cannot make good seasons nor entirely prevent the effects of bad ones, but it can very much modify them. Whoever can manage to save his bees in bad seasons, is sure

of large profits in good ones. Some men have made a great
deal of money from bees. Why cannot any one? Three-
fourths of the bees that perish might be saved with proper
care. If two-thirds of the bees that swarm were kept alive,
there would be fifty thousand in this (Harrison) county, in a
very few years. There are probably four thousand in it now.
There is but little danger of overstocking the country.
Most authors agree on this. In European countries to have
one and two thousand hives in one apiary is common. The
six hundred within two miles of this place seem to do equally
as well as where there are only a dozen in one place. At
any rate there will be no danger from starvation where there
are not more than two or three hundred kept. But independent of profits, it will pay all lovers of nature to keep
them for the pleasure of watching and studying them.
They add materially to the attractions of a home.

It has been suggested that our stock of bees has become
enfeebled in constitution, and inclined to run out. The introduction of Italian Bees and crossing the breed seems to
remedy that evil. Doubtless very many of the processes and
manipulations recommended, will be objected to by many on
the ground that they are not natural ; that every dis-
turbance of them, or change of their natural course is neces-
sarily injurious. This seems rather plausible. But on re-
flection we find that it is only by modifying, changing and
controlling the course of the nature of things that we are enabled to appropriate the advantages of them. It must be
done judiciously. This is the only limit. Hiving a swarm
of bees, taking a box of honey, robbing a hen's nest, killing
a calf, and appropriating its food, and all the processes by
which we derive benefit from our domestic animals, are artificial. As the larger portion of bee-keepers yet use the
common open bottom bee-hive, when I speak of any operation with the hive, reference is always had to this kind of
hive, except where other kinds are expressly named.

BEES.

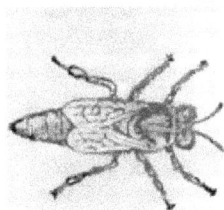

QUEEN.

DRONE.

WORKER.

BEES are almost our only domesticated insect, and aside from their utility, possess many charms for the naturalist. These charms are derived from the variety and beautiful adaptation of their instincts to the ends for which they were created. Their industry, frugality, disposition to defend their homes against their enemies, their mode of propagating their species, their mechanical skill in constructing their combs, depositing honey and pollen, their care of their young, the production and destruction of drones at the proper seasons, their economy of animal heat in their hive, the means by which they know their home and where to find their honey, their ready recognition of the members of their own family, their means of conveying intelligence to one another so as to secure perfect unity of action, their collecting the most delicious of sweets from the most beautiful objects in nature,—all conspire to make them an almost necessary appendage to every home.

The common honey bee is not indigenous to our country, but was imported at an early period in our history. It has never been able to pass over the Rocky Mountains, but has been shipped to the Pacific States within the last twelve years. The Indian calls it the white man's fly, and when bees begin to appear, sorrowfully packs his wigwam and bids adieu to his familiar hunting grounds and the graves of his forefathers.

The bee moth or worm first appeared in the East about sixty years ago, but it is now found as generally as the bee.

About twenty thousand, or from four to five pounds of bees, make a good swarm. Drones are the male bees, and sometimes there are several thousand of them in a hive, and sometimes nono at all. Queens and workers are females. The queen (there is but ono in a hive) lays all the eggs. She ordinarily, in the strong colonies, commences about the first of January, laying at first but a few dozen each day in the centre of the hive, where the bees all cluster to keep warm ; (for it is necessary that they should keep up nearly blood-heat all winter). As the weather becomes warmer the number of the eggs laid gradually increases until about the first of May, when the number laid daily amounts to a thousand or more. And thus she continues to lay until the honey-gathering begins to diminish in August. The number of eggs laid diminishes gradually until in October, when it ordinarily ceases altogether, and the queen has one or two months' rest.

But some seasons bees do not swarm at all. What becomes of so many bees if a thousand are produced daily, and there are no more in the hive in the fall than in the spring ? They die. The life of the worker will not average more than four months, whilst that of the queen is from three years to five years.

"Like leaves on trees the race of bees abound,
Now green in youth, now withering on the ground ;
Another race the spring or fall supplies,
They droop successive, and successive rise."—EVANS.

In midsummer, bees will venture out for honey at all hazards, exposing themselves to storms and birds, wearing out their wings, so that destruction is rapid. I have known whole colonies to perish thus in six weeks, and an entirely new stock to take their place. This is why a colony will soon dwindle to nothing if they have no queen to replace their loss.

"The race and realm from age to age remain,
And time but lengthens with new links the chain."—BEVAN.

Bees will not leave their hive on account of the loss of their queen, except in the case of a young swarm, for the first day or two after being hived, but will remain and perform their ordinary duties with a somewhat abated energy until they all die. We have no bees in the fall that we have in the spring except the queens. In the winter season bees remain quiet in their hives, and the loss is small, so that most of the bees we had in the fall we have in the spring.

A queen is hatched and fully developed in sixteen days from the time the egg is laid; a worker or common bee requires twenty-one days, the same as a chicken. Drones require twenty-four days to mature. The queen lays all the eggs that produce queens, drones, and workers. There is a small portion of comb in the side or in the lower end of almost every hive, but especially in large hives, that is devoted to producing drones. It is known by the cups or cells being larger than those devoted to rearing workers. Measuring the diameter of these cells, you find it to be one-fourth of an inch—that is four to the inch, making sixteen cells to the square inch, or counting both sides, thirty-two young drones can be reared in one square inch of comb. The part devoted to rearing workers gives twenty-five cells to the square inch, or fifty young workers to the cubic inch, the cells being a half inch deep. So uniform is the size of the cells devoted to rearing brood, that some mathematicians have insisted on using them as a standard of measure.

Cells in which queens are reared are separate and distinct structures, generally about an inch long, in size and shape bearing a striking resemblance to a peanut. They are generally built on the edge or lower end of a comb, the end of the cell projecting downward; that is, the queen stands on her head until she cuts her way out and is hatched. Even from this rude description any one may easily recognize these cells on turning the common box hive bottom side up. When the queen is hatched the bees destroy her cell; so that when I am asked to show where the queen stays, I am at a loss for an answer, she having no throne or palace, but is content to make her home in any place in the hive where eggs are to be laid, which is always in the centre and lower parts of the combs—in the height of the breeding amounting to more than one-half of the combs in a medium sized hive, and may be known by their being darker than the combs that are used entirely for honey.

Bees ordinarily have but one queen in the hive, and she is the mother of the whole colony. When they swarm she goes with the new colony, leaving no queen in the old hive; but she leaves an abundance of worker eggs; from these eggs the bees remaining in the hive will proceed to rear for themselves a queen. Three-fourths of the bees, old and young, generally leave with the swarm; one-fourth, most of them less than a week old, remaining in the old hive. The old hive will then contain perhaps twenty thousand eggs and young bees, the eggs hatching daily for three weeks. Bees do not hatch by litters, but are hatching every minute of summer.[*]

Yes, I said the old colony will raise a queen from a common egg, as men make a president of a common citizen. Queens and workers are all females; but workers seem like other animals not yet arrived at puberty.

> "But of all customs which the bee can boast,
> 'Tis this that claims our admiration most:
> That none will hymen's softer joys approve,
> Nor waste their spirits in luxurious love:
> But all a long virginity maintain,
> And bring forth young without a mother's pain."—VIRGIL.

By what means do the workers convert a common egg to a perfect queen? We know of no means except that she is developed in a much larger cell, and receives a different kind of jelly or paste for food, and receives six times as much of it, thus developing in sixteen days to a perfect queen, instead of twenty-one days necessary to develop a worker. Sometimes queen cells are started before the swarm leaves. Most invariably the queen will hatch in eleven days from the time the cell is started. Why so? Because they usually take eggs that are five or six days advanced.

An egg is nearly the size and the shape of a timothy seed. When three days old it is hatched and becomes a worm, maggot or larva of the young bee, when it is supplied with a limpid jelly, made of honey, bee-bread, and water. After a few days they deposit enough food to develop it; it is then sealed over and left till it is able to eat its way out.

I said when the swarm left, the old colony proceeded to rear themselves another queen; but they usually rear from five to fifteen; and why, since only one is needed in the hive? The old queen is gone, and they have now none to lay eggs in case an accident should befall the one they are trying to raise. In such case they would soon dwindle to nothing. If they do not take the eggs before they are eight days old they can

---

[*] The eggs of a bee hatch out in three days. From that time until they are capped over and assume the shape of a bee, are called worms, maggots, or larvæ. From the time they assume the shape of a bee and are capped over until they leave the cell, they are called chrysalis, nymph, or pupa. The term brood includes each and all the stages of development. The term hatch is applied both to the changing of an egg to a larva, and the nymph coming from the cell. Royal cells are cells in which queens are reared.

not convert them into queens. I never, but once, knew a colony to rear a queen from brood more than eight days old. In this case, I presume, the development of the brood was retarded by cold. Bees use all precaution to prevent failure to raise a queen, and therefore raise a number of them. One hatching out first seeks to destroy all rivals; passing through the hive she eats a hole in each royal cell, destroying the embryo queen, leaving the workers to carry out the corpse. Should two hatch simultaneously, they will meet and a battle ensues, the victor becoming sovereign of the hive. It is not left to the workers to destroy the supernumerary queens, for some would be killing at one side and some at another side of the hive, and thus all the queens might be destroyed. But the surviving queen will not destroy herself. These young queens begin to leave their cells about the tenth or eleventh day after the swarm has left. If the sources of honey are now good, the weather favorable, and the hive rather populous, the bees may decide to give off another swarm, and consequently not allow the newly hatched queen to destroy the embryo queens. She becomes dissatisfied with the restriction upon her royal prerogative, and to show her displeasure, commences to pipe or bark, the queens in the cells replying as well as their confined positions will permit.

The experienced bee-keeper, from the eighth to the twelfth evening after the first swarm, puts his ear to the entrance of the hive, and if he hears the piping of the queens, expects certainly to have a second swarm the next day if the weather be fair. The piping noise is of course not heard before the first swarm. When the second swarm is gone other young queens will hatch, and a third swarm issues two or three days after; thus giving off nearly all the bees of the hive, and leaving but little brood to hatch. Such a hive is poorly protected, and in August or September is likely to be destroyed by moth or robbers. It is to be noted that all the young queens in the hive will be hatched within sixteen days of the time the first swarm comes off. There is, consequently, no danger of any more swarms from that colony, that season, no matter how they may cluster outside the hive. Several queens may hatch out the same day, and be given off with the after-swarms; but they are soon all killed except one for each swarm. If eight days after the first swarm issues, all the queen cells except one were destroyed, it would save

1*

the old stock from exhaustion, and prevent annoyance from weak and after-swarms. An artificial swarm may be made by driving two-thirds of the bees with the queen, into the new hive, setting it on the old stand, and moving the old hive away a rod or more. The latter will proceed to rear a queen in the same manner as a colony from which a swarm had issued naturally. If a colony is queenless and have no eggs from which to rear a queen, it can be supplied with comb containing eggs from another hive.

FERTILIZATION OF THE QUEEN.

The impregnation of the queen never takes place in the hive, but always in the open air, on the wing; sometimes as far as two or three miles from home. The queen generally flies abroad for this purpose in the middle of the day, when she is about a week old. At this time of day, in fair weather, the drones flying are numerous, so that there is but little doubt of her meeting them on her first flight, although she sometimes has to fly out several times. She will commence laying in two or three days after impregnation, and, strange to say, *will continue fertile during life—four or five years—* without further intercourse with the drones.

In practice, if a queen is hatched so defective in wings that she cannot fly, I kill her at once, knowing that she will never be of any service in the hive. But if once fertilized, her wings may be cropped, or she confined in a hive where no drone can have access to her. She will continue to lay, without interruption, during life. I will here state a fact which seems a strange anomaly : If anything happens by which a queen's impregnation is prevented, she will eventually commence laying, but all such eggs produce drones, whether laid in worker or drone cells. Also, in some cases where a colony is for a long time queenless, *some of the workers will lay a few eggs, but such eggs, like the eggs of an unfertilized queen, will produce nothing but drones.*

HOW TO RAISE QUEENS ARTIFICIALLY.

After the queen is fertilized she never leaves the hive except with the swarm, but continues moving gracefully over the comb, depositing eggs in the bottoms of the empty cells

The bees constantly back out of her way as she moves along, and offer warm honey from their proboscees, of which she frequently partakes. There is a circle of bees always around her, with their heads toward her, each one in its turn advances and touches her with its antenæ or horns; backing out of the circle it crosses horns with its nearest neighbor, and this last with its neighbor, and so on, keeping up a constant communication throughout the hive, showing that the queen is there all right. Should the queen be removed from the hive, the whole colony will soon become aware of the loss, and run confusedly through and on the outside of the hive, inquiring by this same crossing of horns for their absent queen, communicating the sad intelligence of the loss of their royal mother. Should she be returned to them, all would soon be quiet again ; but if not returned, they would, in a few hours, commence rearing themselves a new queen.

A queen may be known by the length of her body, which is much greater in length than that of the worker. Her color is more of a yellowish cast. Unlike the worker, she has no baskets on her thighs, formed of curved hairs, for carrying bee-bread. Her sting is longer than the worker's, yet she can not be induced to use it on anything except a rival queen ; but put two queens under a glass tumbler and a desperate battle may be witnessed.

ITALIAN BEES.

The United States Government being aware that all our valuable domestic animals, including horses, cattle, sheep, hogs, fowls, &c., were originally imported from other countries, and that by repeated importations of the varieties of each, the value of our stock has been improved incalculably ; and learning from Virgil, as well as others, both ancient and modern writers, that the Italian bees were not only more beautiful, but possessed many qualities much superior to the Common or German bees, they concluded that true economy demanded that they should import some of this variety ; accordingly they did so at great expense, through the agency of the Patent Office Department. Such is their value that they are now being rapidly disseminated ever every portion of our country. When first introduced a single queen was valued at five hundred dollars ; but now there are so many importers of them that the price is much reduced, The abdomen of the bee is composed of six segments or rings. The Italian variety is distinguished by having the first three segments under the wings yellow. The abdomen of the queen is nearly all of a golden yellow. These bees are more prolific and vigorous than the German variety, and give off earlier and larger swarms. They are more industrious and work more freely on the second or seed crop of clover and other flowers on which the common bees do not work; consequently, in bad seasons, they are rich in honey, while the other variety are starving; and strong, vigorous colonies always protect themselves best against moths and robbers.

Pure Italians are less inclined to sting than the Black bee. They are no more inclined to rob than other bees, if they are so much so. The queen being very yellow is more easily distinguished than in the German variety. Correspondents of our agricultural journals speak in glowing terms of these bees. Dzinzon, the great German bee-keeper, says the profits of his Apiary have been doubled since their introduction. The almost universal testimony of those with whom I am acquainted who have tested them, is strongly in their favor. Thomas Groves, who lives near this place, tells me that his Italian hive last spring gave off four swarms; his first swarm swarmed twice, and two of the after-swarms swarmed, making eight swarms this season as the increase from the original stock. Two of the swarms went to the woods; the remaining six and the mother colony are all well supplied with honey for winter, besides making him eighty pounds of surplus or box honey to spare. Estimating his six new colonies at ten dollars each, and his honey at twenty-five cents per pound, make eighty dollars credit to the parent stock. Others mention cases nearly as good. Bees apparently alike good, differ largely in productiveness, so there are cases where Italian bees, sitting side by side with the natives, produce less than they, but this is a rare exception.

HOW TO PROPAGATE ITALIAN BEES, AND TO CONVERT COMMON BEES TO ITALIAN

Queens are the mothers of the colonies. To control the queens is to control the stock. If a queen is given to a colony when they already have one, they will kill the stranger;

but if a colony has had its queen removed a few hours or days, they will be anxious to receive another; and if they have access to worker eggs will rear a number of young ones.

If the bee-keeper will take his pure Italian queen from her hive, the colony will proceed to rear from five to ten young ones, which will commence hatching in ten or eleven days from the time the queen is removed. One or two of these should be left in the hive for their use. At the expiration of eight or nine days, the remainder may be cut out, leaving a little comb with the cell to prevent bruising it. As many native queens may now be removed from their hives as there are of these cells, and one of the cells immediately put in each hive, having previously cut a hole in a brood comb to receive the cell. The queen will most likely emerge from the cell in two or three days, and a week after this fly abroad to mate with the drones, and in two or three days more will commence laying eggs, which will hatch in three weeks; and usually in two or three months from this time all the native stock will be dead, and the Italians in their place. These young queens will be apt to mate with the kind of drones most abundant when they fly out; and if these be native, of course the progeny will not be pure, except that the *drones from all such queens will be pure Italian;* so that if, after this, pure queens are reared in such an apiary, or bee-yard, they will be quite certain to mate with pure Italian drones. These hybrids may then be removed and pure ones inserted in their stead. If, having removed a queen and inserted a cell, the latter fails to hatch, the colony will rear a native queen from their own brood.

To remove the queen, if in a movable comb-hive, open the hive and she can be found on the combs. If in a common box hive, invert the hive and set an empty one of nearly the same size on top of this; then by rapping on the lower hive the bees will be driven into the upper box When the bees begin to run up, the top box may be leaned to one side and search be made for the queen, as the bees go up the side of the hive. But, if she is not thus found, the hive may be set on its stand, and the bees shaken out on a sheet in front of it, and hived as when they swarm. The queen may then be found as the bees run into the hive.

Another mode of rearing a queen, is to destroy the queen of a hive of natives. Eight days after this open the hive and

destroy all the queen cells they have started, then give them
some comb containing brood. From this a number of royal
cells will be produced to be distributed to other hives in eight
or nine days. If a movable comb hive is used, a comb containing eggs and larvæ from the Italian may be exchanged
for a comb of the queenless colony ; or two or three pieces of
comb, from three to five ·inches long, and an inch or more
wide, containing eggs and larvæ, just hatched, may be inserted in holes cut in the brood combs of the queenless colony
to receive them, like cap-stones over doors and windows, leaving a half-inch or more space below them to give room for
the cells to be built downwards.

I am asked: "Do you pretend to say that any person may
thus manipulate bees without being stung almost to death ?
Can bees *really* be handled with any degree of safety?"

I must say, I think no one can handle bees much without
being stung some; and there are few whom it hurts so seriously
to be stung, that it is not wise in them to engage in bee
culture, at least without being well protected by a bee-
dress. "I presume that the man who can close his mouth on
a handful of bees, or swarm a colony on his face, can handle bees with impunity." No, there is but little difference in
people's liability to be stung. There is much in the motions
and manner of approaching bees: but a colony once enraged
will master the most skillful. The taking of a box of honey
unskillfully, or carelessly leaning a hive to one side, will oc-
casion more stinging than the most heroic feats in handling
bees, when practised with a little judgment. It is easier to
control a whole colony intelligently, than a single bee ig-
norantly. Stinging is instinctive and necessary to these little creatures, as it is a protection against their enemies, and
the indiscriminate handling of their keepers. It would not
do at all to have bees that would not sting. But, surely any
one with a knowledge of the condition under which bees do
sting, and some practised skill in their management, will be
able to perform all necessary operations with but little
danger.

It is not right to suppose that bees are always on the alert
for an opportunity to sting. They sting in defence of the
home and life of the colony. In stinging the bee loses its
stinger and with it its life. While away from home or collecting
honey from flowers, bees do not voluntarily sting. Bees that

I have had in hives on the side of the pavement during two summers, where footmen passed every few moments, never stung. Yet bees keep a special guard over their homes, and anything they understand to be an attack on their hives, they will resent with desperation. Breathing on them is offensive—any striking or other quick motions will induce an assault; but more especially jarring the hives, even the most trifling, will drive them forth in great fury; and the poisonous odor emitted by a single sting, makes it doubly sure that others will follow in large numbers and with increased ferocity, until the provoking cause is removed. Bees once enraged sometimes remain so for days or weeks. When among bees always move quietly; if attacked hold the head down and place your hands over your face. Bees instinctively know where you most hate to be stung. If stung, make no sudden motion; withdraw the sting as quickly as possible, for it continues to work in deeper and inject more poison. If the bee-keeper is going to open his hive of bees, or handle them, in any way that would anger them, he should prepare himself with a roll of cotton rags of the size of an ear of corn, rolled so tightly as not to blaze when one end is fired. With this roll burning approach the hive and blow smoke into it until the bees have gotten up the full hum of retreat and submission. You may then proceed to handle them. If they rally and show signs of fight, give them more smoke. It will seem to them that they are to lose all their stores, and to save some, they will gorge themselves with honey, and bees filled with anything sweet rarely sting. This is one reason why they sting so little when they swarm, as they fill themselves before leaving the hive. Feeding bees with water well sweetened with sugar, a while before operating, will keep them in a good humor. Bees are much less inclined to sting while they are collecting honey than at other times. A bee hat of wire-cloth or bobbinet is a good protection for the face and neck; and gum-elastic gloves will protect the hands. Drawing the boots over the pants protects the ancles and legs.

I have little faith in the remedies for bee stings, yet the popular ones are numberless. I presume ammonia, or hartshorn, soda, or camphor are among the best.

HONEY IS NOT MADE BY BEES.

Bees do not make honey—they only collect it. Their honeysack is not a chemical laboratory for manufacturing sweets. If bees are fed on Cuba honey it will be found but slightly altered in the combs. If you feed dissolved sugar, dissolved sugar will be found in the cells. If bees collect honey from dogwood or tobacco bloom, we get an unpleasant or bitter honey. Buckwheat yields a dark-colored honey. White clover yields a beautiful, transparent honey, which when first gathered, is almost as limpid as water. It is left uncapped until the water evaporates, and then sealed air tight,—thus preventing souring and candying.

Bees do not collect honey from filthy slops as many suppose. They frequent such places most in the spring of the year for water, when they need it for their young. Their instincts lead them to obtain their drink from ooze or moist earth, instead of streams or bodies of water, whereby in their excessive eagerness they would be drowned.

Bees lick or suck their honey from the flowers, with their proboses, until their honey sack, which is in their abdomen, is filled. They then disgorge this into a cell and return for another load.

When honey is scarce in the vicinity of the apiary and abundant elsewhere, they sometimes fly three or four miles in search of it, yet they collect larger quantities if it can be found within a half mile. Perhaps four-fifths of the honey collected is from white clover, and most of this is collected in four or five weeks, about the swarming time. The presence of abundance of flowers is no sure evidence that honey is being collected. As soon as honey-gathering begins to diminish, after swarming, much more surplus need not be expected that season, although they may, whilst the flowers last, continue to collect enough for present use, to save what is stored away for winter.

Buckwheat used to be considered a great source of honey, but it is very uncertain, and for seven or eight years past has yielded almost nothing.

Willow and maple are the first to yield food for bees, and are excellent to feed their young and give them an early start. Fruit bloom comes next, and often assists largely in filling the lower chamber of the hive. Next comes locust and white clover. The locust yields freely but lasts only a few days. Poplar and linden or baswood are excellent, but they are becoming scarce in most localities. In the Western States prairie bloom is a great source of honey.

Is there such a thing as "Honey Dew?" In reality, I think there is no such thing as honey falling from the atmosphere in the form of dew, as I have never known any one to find it on the ground, fences, rocks, or any place except on the leaves of trees and plants, or on something immediately under them. Several persons have told me that during last summer they saw it on currant leaves. It is often seen on the leaves of the hickory tree. From all I can learn, I conclude it is a sweet substance that oozes from the leaves of trees and plants where they have been punctured by such insects as the aphis or plant louse; or from an over luxuriant growth have burst the stems of leaves. When this has dried on the leaves the dew moistens it and enables the bees to collect it. If any one can give me authenticated facts (through the newspaper or otherwise) confirmatory of a different theory from the above, I would be glad to have them.

The longer honey is left in the hive the darker it becomes. Old honey is more wholesome than new; but it is not necessary for the comb to be black in order to be old. Honey and honey comb are different things. New honey is often stored in old, dark combs. Honey in white combs may be kept white. When liquid honey is exposed to the air, it soon becomes candied in cold weather; and if liquid honey is allowed to stand in a vessel with combs the whole mass will become candied. To prevent this, fit some cross strips of wood two or three inches from the bottom of the jar or vessel that is to contain the honey—then set the combs on their edges on these sticks, and all the liquid honey will settle below. A better way is to keep the honey in the box in which it was made until ready to use.

POLLEN, OR BEE-BREAD.

The impregnating substance of the flowers of fruits and plants, is a kind of farina or flour, in consistence much the same as rye flour, and which when gathered by the bees, is called Pollen, or Bee-bread. It is collected from ragweed,

dandelion, pumpkin, and many other kinds of flowers. Bees
serve an important end here in carrying pollen on their
bodies from flower to flower, thus making them fertile and
crossing the varieties.   In this there is a notable adaptation
of means to ends in the Divine economy, that, apparently to
preserve the integrity of each species of plants, a bee will
always complete its load from whatever plant it commences
on, regardless of the scarcity of the flowers on which it commences or the abundance of others around them.   They collect their pollen in little pellets or balls on the sides of their
legs, and when it is dry they carry an additional portion by
dusting it over their bodies.   Bees eat a small portion of bee-
bread themselves, but it is mainly used for feeding their
brood, and is always placed in close proximity to the brood,
so that the bee-keeper who wishes his table honey free from
bee-bread must have it made as far as possible from the
brood.

Bees can subsist during winter and spring without bee-
bread ; but they do not seem to prosper nearly as well.   Rye,
or even wheat flour, may be fed advantageously to bees in
the spring, before they are able to collect it from natural
sources.   Place the flour in shallow boxes, set in the sunshine, in a calm place, near the bees, where they will delight
to roll themselves in it.

PROPOLIS.

Propolis is a kind of paste or bee glue, used by the bees to
glue cracks in their hives.   Their hives are sometimes almost
lined with it.   Hives are sometimes so glued to their stand
that it requires considerable force to remove them.   It seems
to be gathered from the buds of various kinds of trees, as the
balm-of-gilead, poplar, &c.   When bees have access to newly
varnished furniture, they will collect varnish for the same
purpose.   The fact that bees have sometimes been known
to alight on the coffins of their keepers, has doubtless given
rise to the superstition that they are aware of his death and
have thus joined the family in mourning his departure.

HONEY-COMB.

Combs are used for storing honey, for nests for the young,
and as a warm harbor for the bees in winter. It is not made of

the yellow bee-bread that bees carry on their legs, as many suppose, but it is an animal secretion from the body of the bee as milk is from the cow. Bees seem possessed of the power of producing it whenever needed. The substance used to manufacture it is honey or some other saccharine matter. Enclose a colony of bees in a hive and feed them honey or dissolved sugar, and they will construct combs and fill them with the same. Remove these and continue to feed them and they will construct more combs. It is generally calculated that it will require about twenty pounds of honey to make one pound of comb, so that to feed bees to induce them to make combs is rather expensive; and it is good economy to save all the combs possible; hence the impropriety of patronizing the peddler of a cheap compound of sugar, Cuba honey, honey and water, or anything else to feed bees for the purpose of constructing combs and storing honey for market. It will take twenty pounds of the compound to make one pound of comb, and in the process of storing the honey, perhaps, one-third is consumed by the bees; and when it is stored, the honey, as will be seen by referring to the article on honey, will be of the same quality as the article fed; so that it would be far better economy to eat the article instead of feeding it to the bees The small scales of wax of which the combs are composed ooze out between the rings on the under side of the abdomen of the bee. These small pieces are taken and worked into the structure of combs. Many of these small scales which have been dropped by the bees, may generally bo found on the bottom board the next morning after a colony has been hived.

A certain temperature in a hive is necessary in order that wax may work well, so that a large number of bees is always necessary in a hive to keep up heat, consequently, if swarms are very small they can spare but few bees to go abroad to labor.

Bees, when left to their own instincts, cluster in the top of the hive, and most generally start about eight combs in a hive twelve inches wide, being built perpendicular and parallel to each other, the edges of the combs being fastened to the sides of the hive, but no comb fastened to another.

Combs built in surplus honey boxes will be more irregular in shape, and are generally thicker than in the main chamber; and when the cells are very deep they are curved

upward tho better to retain the honey. The combs in tho
side and top of tho hive are filled with honey, and when
capped over aro about one-fourth of an inch apart. The
middle and lower ends of the combs are occupied by brood,
and when filled are one inch thick; when emptied of young
bees they are still less, leaving a space of about five-eighths
of an inch. This is the winter quarters for the bees.

BEES CAN ONLY KEEP UP THE NECESSARY TEMPERATURE
OF BLOOD HEAT IN MIDWINTER BY HOVERING IN A COM-
PACT CLUSTER. If all the combs in the hive were sheets of
cold honey, only one-fourth of an inch apart, they would
afford the bees rather cool lodgings, and they would certainly
perish. But as the young bees are about through hatching
by the first of November, the bees will crawl into the empty
cells in the middle of the hive and fill the space between tho
combs, thus making a compact cluster presenting but little
surface to the cool air; and empty combs being non-con-
ductors of heat, they are enabled to economize their heat
most admirably; hence it may be seen a colony may have too
much honey to winter well. A good, populous colony will,
in this way, if kept dry, endure the rigors of the most severe
winters in the United States. In warm days they will carry
some honey in from the sides and top of the hive, and deposit
it in the cells in the centre of the cluster, where they may
have access to it in severe weather, to prevent venturing out
in the cold parts of the hive for it. This gives rise to the
idea that bees eat most in warm weather. But there seem to
be cases where the extreme cold is so protracted, that the
bees, having consumed all the honey deposited in the cluster, and there being frost and ice on all parts of tho comb
containing the honey, they may starve in tho cluster with
plenty of honey around them. The bees on the outside of
the cluster will change places with those further in, and in
extremely cold weather the whole colony will resort to an
agitating motion to generate heat. Visit a large apiary in a
very cold, calm morning, and the hum may be heard two or
three rods; in moderate weather they cannot be heard.
This discomfort and increased activity of the bees seems to
create a greater demand for food. As a matter of economy
some protection should be necessary. When the combs are
entire from top to bottom, with no holes in the centre of them
to admit of tho passing of the bees from the outside to the

centre, a sudden cold spell will freeze a number of them between the outside combs. Holes made through the centre of these combs in the fall, would remedy the evil. In common hives a hole could be bored through them ; in movable comb hives the combs could be lifted out and holes cut in them. I said a populous hive of bees could endure a great amount of cold if kept dry inside. Bee-keepers have gone to their hives in a warm day, immediately succeeding a cold spell, and found water running down the inside of the hive, and standing in puddles on the bottom board, and have wondered where so much water came from, as their hives were well covered. Bees are constantly perspiring, and the perspiration rises and settles on the sides and top of the hive and on the combs. Turn a box hive bottom up after a night's hard freezing, and the combs inside of the hive will be found covered with frost. If the freezing should continue several weeks, the amount of ice would be considerable. In the winter of '55 and '56, hard freezing continued two or three months, until in many cases, where there was no upward ventilation, there was moisture congealed to the amount of from a pint to a quart. One warm day thawed it and it ran among the combs and bees, and the same evening there set in a hard freeze, and many colonies of bees perished. It is estimated that one-half of the bees in the State of Ohio died that winter, although generally rich in honey. Hives that had holes in the top and empty boxes set over them, or were otherwise ventilated, fared much better.

PREPARING TO WINTER.

It is not good economy to attempt to winter bees not amply supplied with honey to last them until the flowers appear in the spring, for winter and spring feeding is generally very unsatisfactory ; and to have bees die in the spring, after eating fifteen or twenty pounds of nice honey, is quite a disappointment. Difference in colonies, and different seasons, and the manner of wintering, variously affect the amount required by a colony. It is perhaps best to have a rule not to commence wintering a colony with less than twenty-five pounds of honey, although it is seldom a colony will consume so much as that ; but it is unsafe to run them too close. On the first of November, unless the combs in a hive are very old,

if it weighs thirty-five pounds over and above the weight of
the empty hive, it may be supposed to contain honey enough
to winter.

EQUALIZING STOCKS FOR WINTER.

An apiarian, with a considerable number of bees, will, in
the fall, have some colonies that are rich in honey but scarce
in bees by overswarming, loss of queen, or other misfortune.
Other hives will have enough bees, but only from one to
twenty pounds of honey and but little bee-bread, the remainder having proper proportions of honey, bee-bread and
bees.   These defective colonies should have been avoided by
preventing so much swarming (see article on swarming); but
in this as in many other things, we do not always accomplish
what we should, or might accomplish.   The question is how
to make the most of things as they are.   As soon as honey-
making is over, and the bee-keeper finds that he has a number of such defective stocks, he must lessen the number
of them by driving the bees that have almost no honey
into those that have an abundance of it, but are scarce in
bees ; and uniting the bees and honey of others in order to
make them sufficiently strong and rich.   But before I show
how this is done, I must show how bees may be agreeably
united.

BEES ARE JEALOUS OF FOREIGNERS, and before such can
enjoy the full privilege of citizenship they must comply with
their naturalization laws ; and one of these laws is, that they
must come in well loaded with honey.   When bees are gathering honey freely, and a bee misses its own hive and pro-
poses to enter another, if it is well loaded with honey it is
permitted to enter and domicil with them.   So, if you have
two colonies, the one very strong and the other very weak,
change the relative positions of the hives, putting the strong
one on the stand of the weak one, and the weak one on the
stand of the strong one.   The bees from the strong hive will
go out in great numbers for honey, not noticing as they leave
that they have been moved, and on returning will enter the
weak colony.   Being filled with honey they will be kindly
received..   On entering they feel lost on finding themselves
in a strange family, and will immediately hurry out to rectify
the mistake ; but on looking around in vain for something

more like home than the hive now occupying the old familiar
spot, they will return and soon be at work as eagerly as ever.
A few from the weak stock will, in the same manner, join
the strong one. In this way colonies may be made equal in
strength. I have known colonies of native bees, brought
many miles in the winter, into the neighborhood of Italian
bees, and before swarming time a considerable number of
Italians would be in the native hive, thus showing that they
do neighbor some.

Ordinarily, when bees are not making honey, if a stranger
attempts to enter a hive, it is roughly examined, and if it can
not show the proper credentials, it is ejected forthwith. But
the common mode of recognition is by the sense of smell.
When I set my bees out in the spring, having had a great
many of them together in a close cellar all winter, they have
acquired the same odor. I can then take bees from one hive
and put them into another, or unite them as I please, without
producing a conflict.

If it is desired to unite two colonies, if in open bottomed box
hives, set one on top of the other, having holes in the top of the
lower hive, which should be covered with wire cloth or other
porous material to keep the bees apart for a week or ten days.
The odor passing from the lower hive, through these holes,
gives them all the common scent of one family. The coverings of the holes should then be removed and they will unite
amicably. There might be an opening left in the upper hive
for the bees to pass out and in until the coverings of the holes
in the top of the lower hive are removed. The opening in
the upper hive should then be closed to make the bees go
down into and through the other hive and become one colony.

A speedier way is to unite the bees, then smoke them well
with tobacco, or, more generously, to sprinkle them with water
well sweetened and strongly scented with peppermint or
other essence, which will so obliterate, for the time being,
the natural odor, that neither will know which to fight. If
the bees to be united are in movable comb hives, put the
fullest combs of both hives into one. If they are in
box hives, invert the best one, or the one in which you
wish the bees to remain ; blow a little smoke among the
bees to drive them down off the combs whilst you trim
the ends of the combs square. Having driven the bees out
of the other hive, cut out the combs and put them on their

edges in the first hive, putting the heavy end down as the
hive now stands ; scraps of empty comb or wads of paper can
be placed between the combs to hold them in place until the
bees have fastened them.   Now shake the bees of the other
colony into this, and sprinkle it with your sweet-scented water and cover it over closely except a small entrance for the
bees, and leave it in this position until the combs are all
fastened in the hive, one, two or more weeks.   The bees will
eat the honey out of these newly put in combs first, making
them light, and these combs will be a fine addition to their
stock for the next season.   Two small colonies, if run together, will eat much less than they would if wintered
separately.

WEAK COLONIES SUFFER MOST FROM COLD.

For though they may not freeze, a too long exposure to a
low temperature produces dysentery ; and bees are of such a
cleanly nature, that when their bodies are distended with excrement they cannot retain it;   they will leave the hive
to relieve themselves, even at the risk of perishing.   In this
way colonies are sometimes depopulated in early spring, when
they have been too damp in the winter, or have been too thinly
populated to keep up the necessary heat.   Protracted damp-
ness inside of a hive produces dysentery, as it seems to sour
the honey and chill the bees.   A colony that is suffering with
this disease will generally have the entrance, and sometimes
most of the whole front of the hive, daubed with excrement ;
and if they can not get out, they will so smear the combs,
that death is almost inevitable.   This seems to be the only
disease that prevails amongst bees except Foul-Brood.*

WINTERING.

On wintering bees such a variety of plans have been suggested that the inexperienced are puzzled to determine which
is best.   Some recommend burying them in grain, burying

* This is a disease in which the brood rots in the cells and is fatal to the colony.   If
the bees of other colonies eat honey from the diseased one, it gives them the disease
also.   Many extensive bee-keepers in Germany have lost hundreds of colonies from
this cause ; and in the State of New York, it prevails extensively.   I know of some
cases in Western Pennsylvania.   There is little or none of it in Ohio, and I hope there
never will be.   It has been transmitted by shipment to California.   The cause seems
a mystery.   The remedy is to drive all of the bees of an affected colony into an empty
hive, and render the honey, bringing it to a boil, to purify it for use.

them in the earth, housing them in a room, or keeping them in a cellar; whilst others maintain that it is more natural to leave them out of doors on their stand. I have myself practised all of these plans, and doubt not that bees have been wintered well on each of them. But I do not consider them all alike good; and it would be as well to adopt the best plan at once. What we wish to accomplish is to give comfort to our bees Our cattle, sheep, and bees may all winter in the open air, if they are strong and vigorous and have plenty of food; but they will surely all winter more comfortably and eat less food if somewhat protected. Some wish to keep their bees in a dormant condition during cold weather, like other insects, and thus lessen the consumption of honey, When the bee-keeper succeeds in stupifying his bees by cold for a short time, he will suddenly arrive to the unhappy consciousness that they are past recovery. Bees are different from most other insects in this, that they live in families and cluster together to economize heat in winter, besides being prepared at all times to defend their stores and their young. Out-of-door wintering is subject to the difficulties arising from external cold; and the bright lights and moderate heat inducing the bees to fly out when the weather is yet so cold as to chill them. Besides, the ground around is so wet that they may perish on it; and when fresh snow has fallen and is yet light, bees will alight upon it, and sinking in it will perish. However, if the snow has a crust on it, or has become compact, bees will rise from it as easily as from dry ground. At this present writing, December 18, 1867, I doubt not there are many colonies of bees smothering to death by the rain and snow having frozen closely around the bottom and entrance of hives, making them air-tight. It is not an unfrequent occurrence, that the exhalations from the bees run down the inside of the hive and freezing on the lower edges make them air-tight and smother the bees.

Some of the difficulties to be encountered by in-door wintering, are—keeping them confined too long from water and from emptying themselves; although they will suffer but little from the first of December until the first of March. If they are kept in damp cellars, or buried in damp ground, the combs will mould and the honey sour and disease the bees.

2

VENTILATION.

In whatever manner bees are wintered, care must be taken that they have air, and are kept dry. If any one doubts whether bees can be smothered, let him confine a swarm in an air-tight box for an hour, and shake them occasionally to keep them active, and he will find his bees all dead and as moist as though they had been drenched in water. In hot weather, whilst transporting a strong colony of bees, nothing less than a whole side or end of a common-sized hive covered with a loosely woven cloth or wire gauze is sufficient to secure a colony from smothering; yet when bees are still and cool in the dark, they require but little air. This is evidenced by the fact, as persons of credibility have informed me, that having attempted to smother a colony of bees in the fall of the year by burying them in a chip-yard, after taking all of their honey, in the spring on digging up the chips they found living bees. I have buried several colonies of them together in the ground, in a dry place, covering them first with boards, and then with a layer of straw or fodder, then with ten inches of clay, leaving plenty of openings in the hives, and having a large tube run up through the top to give upward ventilation; but in this case as in damp cellars, the combs are inclined to mould; and being so very closely confined they become unhealthy after being set out in the spring.

What I consider the best in-door arrangement for winter, that I have used, and for this hint I am indebted to M. Quinby, the author of the "Mysteries of Bee-keeping," one of the most valuable and practical of bee-books, is a room partitioned off in a cellar especially for bees. Mine was ten feet square. The walls were made by setting up four inch scantling, nailing boards on both sides and filling between with sawdust, so that the temperature would not be suddenly affected by the external air. It had an opening at the top and another at the bottom for ventilation. These openings were covered with wire cloth to keep out the mice, and shaded with a cloth to keep out the light. It had four tiers of shelves all around, so that the hives could be set on these like store goods. Common hives were inverted on these shelves and left bottom up, that they might be thoroughly ventilated. (It is not necessary to be alarmed about the bees having to stand all winter on their heads.) Movable comb and other hives were left quite open that the exhalations might evaporate. In this way I have kept from sixty to eighty colonies from the first of December until March very nicely. When the mercury is below zero out of doors, in such a room it would be fifty degrees above. I have frequently gone into my bee-room in extremely cold weather, to warm myself by the heat of my bees and listen to their gentle hum.

The amount of honey consumed in these three months, by a colony kept in this manner, averages from eight to ten pounds.

In the absence of such a room, when there are but a few hives to be housed, they could be set in the corner of a dry cellar where there are no decaying vegetables, and where there would be no pounding or motions to jar them in the least; for this always keeps them in motion, and quiet is very essential. It is well also to keep them well covered or shaded, so that not the least ray of light could fall on them. Towards spring, when they begin to feel a strong inclination to fly out to empty themselves, if there come several days of warm weather, and the bees see the light, they will leave their hives and fly to it, and will fail to return.

Care should be taken to set the bees out in a fine day when they can fly without being chilled, at a time when it is supposed that severe freezing is over, generally about the first of March.

When the bees are set out, or at any time that they are disposed to fly in chilly weather, when the ground is wet around the hives or a light snow has fallen, it is advantageous to spread some hay or straw for them to alight upon.

If bees are wintered out of doors, they should always have a small opening in the side of the hive some distance up from the bottom. Such an opening will always prevent suffocation should the hive become frozen air-tight below. The best plan I know for protection on the summer stand, is to set them close together, near the ground. Set up boards to make a box all around them a foot higher than the hives, leaving a space of a foot or more between the boards and the sides of the hives. Into this space and on the top of the hives, pack saw-dust or chaff. If there are holes in the top of each hive and a cap or box set over them, it will help to ventilate and rid them of moisture, as it would rise from the bees into this cover and settle on the sides of it and run out under its edges, instead of running down again amongst the bees. Or, if there were a tube or openings from the top of the hives up into the open air, it would be of some advantage. All should be well sheltered. Bore a hole with an inch auger in the centre of the front of the hive, to which apply a tube. This tube should be long enough to extend through the chaff and will answer as an entrance for the bees and for ventilation. The tube could be made of narrow strips of board, nailed together and secured carefully to the sides of the hive so as to be always opposite the hole in the hive. This could be done by nailing strips of leather to the tube and to the side of the hive, or by a small cross strip fastened to the side of the end of the tube. Drive screws through this strip into the hive. Be careful to keep this tube always open. In the spring lay them aside for future use.

FEEDING BEES.

Should bees be fed? If so, when? How much? With what? What objects are accomplished by it?

I think that it is really good economy to spend some money for feed, sometimes. "What!" I have heard it said in praise of their thrift, that "Bees work for nothing and board themselves." I am often told by bee-keepers, "If my bees do not make honey enough for themselves, they may die." Again: "I have known persons to spend a great deal in feeding bees, and yet they died." Others say, "Feeding often induces robbery and does more harm than good." When it was customary for bee-keepers, in the fall, to kill their richest colonies for their large stores of honey, and their weak ones to save the little they had gathered, and to prevent them from starving, there were fewer bees to die, and there was less feeding to do; but now we wish to save all the bees we can, and there is no remedy for poor stocks but to feed them.

What shall we feed? Honey is the most natural food for bees, but it cannot always be had, and is rather expensive. Cuba, or West India honey is manufactured by bees and imported mainly from the West Indies, and is a good substitute for the domestic honey. Nearly twenty thousand pounds of this honey was purchased within twenty five miles of this town, in the year 1863, for feeding bees. The successes in feeding it was various, owing to the time of year and the skill in feeding. This honey is generally liquid; but if candied, a little water should be added. It should then be brought to the boil, and when cooled the impurities skimmed from the surface. A good article of brown sugar, or still better, white sugar, dissolved in water to near the consistence of honey, and heated, makes a good feed. Maple molasses does very well. Some claim to have fed sorghum to good advantage. This is the cheapest food that can be procured in this region; but I have never succeeded well in feeding it. It is only under the most favorable circumstances that I can induce the bees to eat it; and in some cases it produced dysentery, seriously injuring the bees. Perhaps in such cases it was an inferior article. Food that is in the least sour, is objectionable. However, I would not hesitate to feed a good article of sorghum to strong colonies, when the weather is quite warm. Bees are much more inclined to dysentery in cool weather, and when eating freely, than when eating sparingly.

Sugar candy is best for winter feeding, as it can be placed between the combs directly amongst the bees, so that they will not have to leave their warm cluster to go out into the cold for it. It possesses the advantage of not keeping them excited, as they are when fed liquid sweets; besides it requires much less of it. It possesses an advantage over dry sugar, as the bees seem able to dissolve it, perhaps with a little moisture from their proboscis; whilst dry sugar is very much wasted because they cannot liquify it.

In warm days, in the early spring, before bees commence gathering pollen, an impetus may be given to breeding, by feeding them rye flour, put in shallow boxes and set in the sunshine, in a calm place near the hives, where all may have access to it. There is no danger of exciting robbery, as there is in feeding honey outside of the hive.

There are two objects to be accomplished in feeding, one is to stimulate the bees to rear brood, the other is to keep them from starving.

Strong stocks are an essential to successful bee-keeping. Such guard themselves against worms, robbers, and the cold. They require less attention and make more honey and combs in proportion to their numbers, and consume less honey.

Whoever succeeds in securing strong stocks has satisfactory
results ; whoever keeps weak ones has little but perplexity.
It is especially important that hives should be very populous
during the months of May, June and July, when honey is to
be gathered. The bee-keeper should, therefore, make everything bend to the production of large numbers of bees during
the early part of the season. Strong colonies of bees generally commence breeding about the first of January, the
queen laying a few eggs in the centre of the cluster of bees.
When she has laid a few in one side of the comb, she goes to
the other side and lays a few just opposite. She will then
enlarge the circle of eggs on both sides of the comb, and then
proceed to the adjacent combs on each side of where she has
been laying, and deposit the eggs in the same manner as in
the first comb. She will then return and enlarge the first
circle, and deposit eggs in the empty cells in the centre; for
by this time (if twenty-one days have elapsed), young bees
will begin to have been hatched from them. In this manner
the bees manage to concentrate their heat on the brood.
The more numerous the bees the greater number they
can produce. As soon as they begin to gather honey and
bee-bread, they commence to breed more rapidly, until at the
commencement of good honey-gathering they will be hatching a thousand or more bees each day ; and if the keeper now
has a colony of thirty thousand bees, ten thousand may remain in the hive during the day to do in-door work and keep
the brood warm, whilst the twenty thousand may go abroad
for stores, and will soon have a good stock of surplus honey,
and will give off swarms of bees. The case is quite the re-
verse with weak, starving stocks. It will be the first of
March before they will commence rearing brood, for they
would have neither bees to keep it warm nor honey to feed
it. When they commence collecting honey from fruit trees
and other early bloom, they will commence rearing a goodly
number of bees which will require a considerable amount of
honey. It may then be two or three weeks before white
clover appears, and having commenced to rear their brood,
they will continue to feed and develop it until they have consumed their small stock of honey. Then if they should be
confined to their hives by four or five days cold weather,
they will all perish. Thousands of colonies of bees, in Ohio,
perished last season between fruit bloom and white clover,

in this manner. Should such colonies barely escape death, they will neglect to develop the eggs laid by the queen, until the honey begins to appear again, and before they can be built up strong in bees, the best honey season will be over, and they will have no surplus honey ; nor will they have bees to spare for a swarm ; and in case the honey season proves a bad one they may have but little honey stored for the coming winter.

What is the remedy for such weak, starving colonies? They should be housed where they can keep themselves and their brood warm until the weather admits of their flying. While the bees are in their winter quarters, if they are scarce of honey, they should be fed on sugar candy (white is the best), placed between the combs, in the cluster of bees; they will remain quietly clustered on it, eating as they need, and save their honey without being excited, as they invariably are when fed any liquid sweet.* If the bees are in a box hive, keep it inverted and place the sticks of candy, one, two or three pounds, between the ends of the combs where the bees will collect on it. I will now describe the mode of feeding these when set on their summer stand.

FEED BOX.

Make as many feed boxes as there are colonies to feed. Take a board one-half inch thick, ten or twelve inches long, and five or six inches wide ; nail all around this strips one and a half or two inches wide, thus making a feed-box one or one and a half inches deep. Melt some rosin and beeswax together, taking equal quantities of each, and pour it around in the corners of the box to make it honey-tight. Into this box pour the liquid food, and spread a few shavings or cut straw over the surface of it to keep the bees from miring. If the colony is weak and the combs built only part way down, the feed box might be inserted under the combs and something placed beneath it to raise it up against them where the bees might have the most easy access to it ; but if the

---

* I have made a cheap article of candy by dissolving a good article of sugar, then adding a teaspoonful of cream of tartar to twenty-five pounds of sugar, evaporate the water by boiling until it shows, by cooling in water that it is brittle. Then pour it into shallow pans slightly greased. When partially cooled cut it into slips, or when cold break it to suit. It might be scented, if desired, with mint. It could be clarified with eggs.

hive be full of combs set the feed-box on top of it ; first bor-
ing holes in the honey or top board for the bees to pass up.
Set a cap or box over this to make sure that no bee can get
at the honey except by coming up through the hive.   When
first commencing to feed in this way streak a little of the
food in and about the holes in the top of the hive to coax the
bees up.   If only a little is to be fed it could be done nicely
by pouring it into the empty combs and placing it where it
would be conveniently accessible.   But this is too slow a process when there are many to feed.   Some have fed by satu-
rating bread with honey or maple molasses and placing it
among the bees.   There are worse plans than this as the
bees would seem to eat a portion of the bread as bee-bread.

WHEN TO FEED.

Always feed in the evening after the bees cease flying, that
other bees may not get a taste.   It will generally be all used
up by the next morning, and robber bees will not be tempted
by the odor.

When commencing to feed be determined *that there shall
not be a particle of honey spilled about the hives, where outside bees can get a taste of it; and that no bee shall go into
the hive except at the small hole where the bees usually go out
and in.*   By strictly observing this rule, bees may be fed almost any amount with almost entire certainty that no robbery
will be committed.

Never feed all of your bees together outside their hives,
as the ones that need the least generally get the most, and
the neighboring bees, for a mile or more around, will find the
food nearly as soon as your own; and it excites to robbery,
for the bees will rush in great numbers to obtain the honey,
and when this is consumed they will approach every hive in
the yard and vigorously test their strength to prevent ad-
mittance, and if any one prove inadequate to the task, it is
soon dispossessed of all its stores.

OBJECTS TO BE AIMED AT IN FEEDING.

The first is to save the bees from starvation.   If bees are
fed in winter they must leave their cluster to get it when
they should be entirely quiet.   This puts them in an ab-
normal condition and is not good.   Besides, if the weather

is very cold or the colony weak, they cannot leave the cluster to get it, and will consequently starve when there is plenty of honey by them. Early spring feeding is liable to the same objections. When feeding is resorted to, bees act as though they were collecting honey from natural sources, being aroused to action they eat freely themselves and rear a greater quantity of brood which requires much honey for their sustenance, so that if bees are thus aroused by feeding, then cease for a time, they will continue to feed their brood until their store is exhausted; then if honey is not to be had from flowers for a week or ten days, they will either starve in their hives, or being driven to desperation, will leave and attempt to enter some other one, where they will be mercilessly massacred. They often leave even when they have a pound or two of honey. This always occurs in very fine days, and I think is in part occasioned by annoyance from robber bees, who attempt to enter their hives. If there comes a very warm day in the last of March or on the first of April, in a spring when bees are not well supplied, I always feel certain of being accosted, when I go on the street on the following day, with the inquiry, from bee-keepers of the surrounding country: "Why did the bees all come out of one of my hives yesterday, and attempt to enter another and were killed?" or, "Why did a swarm of some person's bees come yesterday and attempt to enter one of my hives?"

When a colony thus attempts to decamp they should be put back into their hive and then fed regularly every evening until they can collect honey from flowers. It will add to the safety of the hive if the queen's wings are cropped so that she cannot fly, or to have an entrance regulator applied. [See "Entrance Regulator"] If feeding is commenced in the spring it must be continued until the bees can collect from the flowers. But at this time feed sparingly, say a half pound or more daily. If too much is fed they may fill so many of their cells with honey as not to leave sufficient room for brood, and abundance of brood in the spring is more valuable than the same combs filled with honey; so that in some cases in movable comb hives when the breeding chamber is too much filled with honey, it is best to lift out some of the full combs and set empty ones in their place.

But no bee-keeper should depend on winter or spring feeding; for it is most invariably perplexing and unsatisfactory.

2*

But in September, as soon as his bees cease storing honey, ho should examine them, and should feed lavishly all such as have not sufficient to last them until the next honey-making season. I say *feed lavishly for economy's sake*, for when bees are excited by feeding, they will eat freely. Suppose you feed a gill daily, the bees will be likely to consume nearly all of it, but feed them a quart and they will eat but little more than the gill, and will store the remainder in their cells. So, feed them as rapidly as you can get them to carry it away, and have done with the feeding as soon as possible and let them become quiet. If food is given warm they will work much more readily. If the bees are in a box hive and the top close, invert the hive and pour from a pint to a quart of honey over the bees and combs. Leave the hive sitting bottom up until you have done feeding. Cover closely except a small entrance for the bees. Do not fear drowning the bees, they will lick the honey all off from one another, and feel no more annoyed than a flock of geese would by being dashed with a bucket of water. I have had colonies carry off a quart in three or four hours. Feed bees in the best possible manner, and they will not stow away all that is fed them. In the fall of '63, I selected for feeding thirty-three colonies which had almost no honey. I fed them each an average of thirty pounds of Cuba honey, by so doing the average increase in weight was twenty pounds. A little of this additional weight must be allowed for brood, although I caged the queens in some of the hives to prevent their laying.

Feed early in the season that the honey may be stored whilst the weather is warm, so that the wax with which they cap their honey, may be soft, for they cannot seal it over in cold weather, and the uncapped honey is very apt to sour and disease the bees, besides they store much faster in warm than in cold weather.

The advantages of fall feeding are, it can be done quicker, it takes less food, and is then put just where they will need it in cold weather when they cannot be safely fed. A good rule, given by an old author, runs thus: "In the spring feed sparingly; in the fall feed bountifully; in the winter feed none at all."

Another object in feeding is to induce breeding in the spring so that bees may be very numerous when flowers apdear. In our State, I might say, when white clover appears, which is generally about the first of June. Some very experienced bee-keepers recommend feeding bees in the spring even when they have honey enough, in order to induce breeding, even should it be but a tablespoonful a day.

ROBBERY.

My little friends, so industrious and noble in their general behavior, I am almost sorry to say, are sometimes guilty of the heinous sin of robbing their neighbors, and that too in as shameless a manner as is too common amongst a much higher order of beings. The rich and strong prey upon the poor and defenceless, and that without mercy, although the case is not as many supposed that the attacking .party kill those they attempt to rob, and then take the booty. They adopt the modern gentlemanly way of robbing without taking life; the fighting is mostly done by the defendants. However well I may like non-resistance amongst human beings (especially where they are not pushed too hard), I can not but admire a colony that fights well in self-defence, and am not much afraid of their being overcome so long as they resolutely resist. When a colony in a normal condition is attacked, it has sentinels at every entrance to its citadel, and as Quinby expresses it, "every bee has full authority to act as jurors, judges, and executioners," and no mining region lynch-law is more speedily executed than that of these self-instituted sheriffs.

Like other rogues, robber bees are known by their haggard thievish appearance. They do not approach and enter a hive in a confident, self-satisfied manner, but appear agitated and suspicious, and like thieves generally, try to gain entrance in some other way than the regular one. Bees once addicted to robbery seldom or never reform, but retain their thievish propensity. Bees are ordinarily covered with a nice yellow down, which the scuffling incident to robbery, together with other means, sometimes wears off, they then present the appearance of a small black bee, which some have mistaken for a different variety, more inclined to rob than others. Robbery occurs only in the spring and in the fall, or at times when there is no honey to be had from flowers. When bees, as with some more intelligent creatures, when they have nothing to do, the danger is that they will do that which is worse than nothing.

Careless feeding, or honey left where bees can get at it, is generally the first incentive to robbery. In a village like ours, where there are six hundred hives of bees within two miles of the place, it requires caution on the part of every bee-keeper to retain peace among the bees and good will amongst the neighbors. For if one colony is being robbed, the whole neighborhood of bees become excited. I can generally tell when there has been a colony of bees robbed in my neighborhood; for generally, although *one* may commence the depredations, before it is over, many will participate, and they will not be satisfied with emptying one hive, but will test the strength of every colony in the vicinity, keeping all unusually excited, even pouring into the candy shops and penetrating the kitchens and every apartment where there is the odor of sweets, much to the annoyance of the thrifty house-wife in making her jellies and putting up canned fruit. It will sometimes require several days for the excitement to subside, and will remain for a time susceptible to excitement; and woe to the queenless colony at such times when the keeper has not thoroughly fortified it by reducing the entrances to the capacity merely sufficient for exit and return, so that a few sentinels may defend the colony against a large army of invaders. When robbery commences, close all hives to the least capacity for entrance and exit. If a hive is very determinedly attacked, close the entrance so that but a single bee can pass in and out at a time. If they pile on the hive in great numbers, dash cold water on them; this materially abates their rapacity, and gives them a homeward inclination. If they are ungovernable, close the hive entirely and carry it to a cellar or dark cool place, where it should stand two or three days, until the marauding spirit has subsided, then set it out on the stand. When this hive is moved, those sitting next to it are in danger and should be carefully closed. Before any hive is entirely closed it is necessary to have some holes in it, and cover them with wire cloth to prevent smothering. If a weak colony is closed for two or three days with a great many robbers in it, the most of them will remain and add to its strength.

Some persons have told me that when they had a hive attacked, they have carried it first to one side of the house and then to another to evade the robbery, but still they took it! Of course they took it—that was made doubly certain by the moving. Every time the hive was moved a great many bees would leave and return to the old stand and be lost, thus weakening it until ruin was certain; because the robbers would be sure to find them in a very few minutes if left anywhere in the vicinity.

Persons frequently lament to me, that their neighbors' bees attacked and destroyed one, two or three of their best colonies. It is not agreeable to have to dispute honest people's words, yet I always doubt such reports. There is no doubt that they were robbed, but that they were their best. It is probable that at some previous time they had been their best, but they had either swarmed almost all their bees away, or were queenless, or by some other means were rendered unthrifty, and became an easy prey to robbers, which only anticipated their destruction by moth, for such families will generally perish by some means if not helped. The beekeeper in such cases generally sees a good many bees about the entrance, and is thereby deceived, supposing there are also a proportionate number inside.

HOW TO DETECT ROBBERS.

When a colony is seen going out and in late in the evening, after others have ceased to labor, I suspect either that it is robbing or being robbed. If on examination those coming out appear to be full and rather clumsy in taking flight, my doubts of their honesty become strong and I feel myself justified in arresting a few of them on suspicion. And if on tearing them open their honey-sack proves to be gorged with honey, I consider this circumstantial evidence sufficient, and condemn them accordingly.

Then, to detect the headquarters of the clan, sprinkle the bees as they come out with flour, and notice if any of the other hives have white bees entering them. If not, you may conclude they belong elsewhere.

When bees are robbing they are out in the morning before others are, and fly in the evening after others have become quiet.

When robbery commences it should be stopped immediately, as the robbers come stronger and stronger, until they becomo desperate, when they will pile over each other and struggle and fairly squeal to get into the hive. Any operation involving risk from robbery, is best to be commenced in the evening, just in time to be completed before dark. The bees will then have the wasting honey licked up by the morning, and those of them that have been cowed into non-resistance will have time to rally.

Prevention is better than cure. As weak and queenless colonies are the ones always attacked, leave none such unprotected, as they aro always temptations. A hive set up on blocks, that the bees may get in on all sides, is as objectionable as to have a city unfortified in time of war. Bees will not rob while the flowers yield honey freely, but in the spring and fall be careful.

By observing the foregoing rules the bee-keeper need seldom if ever loose bees by robbery.

THE BEE-MOTH.

The bee-moth has the reputation of being the arch-enemy of bees. It first made its appearance in this State about thirty-five years since. For a few years after, its ravages seemed greater than of late years.

Like the fly which deposits its eggs in fresh meat that her young maggots may have plenty of appropriato food, so the bee-moth follows the bee and deposits her eggs on or near the combs, which is the natural food of her larvæ or worms. They never eat honey, but wax exclusively. Honey in the combs is a great hindrance to their progress, and combs immersed in honey would be entirely safe from them.

They will develope from the egg to the full-sized worm in a few days among the empty combs, if the weather is warm. Cold weather retards their development. Eggs may remain in the hive from fall until spring without hatching. This seems to be the manner in which they are preserved over winter, as the moth seldom appears before June.

If empty combs are left exposed to the severe freezing of winter, the moth eggs will generally be destroyed, and the combs can be kept for swarms.

When it is desired to keep empty combs, destroy the eggs and worms in them by placing them in a close box or barrel and smoke them thoroughly with sulphur. One moth will produce a great many worms.

With the help of a magnifying glass I have counted a thousand eggs in one moth. By pulling off the head of a female, I have had it deposit a dozen or two of eggs in a crease of my hand in a few moments.

The killing of one moth the first of June is worth as much as killing a hundred in August. They are still in the day-time and lay their eggs at night By setting dishes containing a mixture of sweetened water and vinegar about the hives, a great number of millers will be attracted to them and drowned.

HOW TO DETECT THEIR PRESENCE IN A HIVE.

If movable frame hives are used, the combs can be lifted out and examined. Otherwise look at the entrance of the hive for their excrements. They can be distinguished from comb-cuttings by their being darker and of a powder appearance.

If the bees are in an open-bottomed hive it could be turned bottom up and examined. In turning a hive bottom up when the combs are new and heavy with honey, be careful to turn it so that the edges of the combs will rest against the side of the hive to prevent their breaking.

If a moth attempts to enter a well-peopled hive, it is attacked by the bees and has to use great agility in getting out of the hive from danger; but if the hive is weak, and it gets past the sentinels, it will go almost where it pleases through the hive, and deposit its eggs among the combs and comb-cuttings at the bottom and in the cracks of the hive.

Worms are found in the most populous families. It has been suggested that as the eggs are small slimy things deposited about the hives, that they adhered to the feet of the bees and are carried up in the hive. I know of no more reasonable way of accounting for their appearance in such hives. I every season open out and examine every comb in hundreds of hives Early in the spring, long before the moths begin to appear, even in the most populous colonies, a considerable number of worms are found, almost invariably in the heart of the hive among the brood, eating their way between the heads of the young bees and the caps of the cells, making themselves a covered winding road, out of sight of the bees. All the young bees they pass over die, so that if one go five or ten inches it will destroy from twenty-five to one hundred young bees. This is why so many dead young bees are thrown out of the hives in the spring of the year. So soon as the worm has eaten enough to develope itself, it will leave the combs and try to get in some crack or under the hive, to spin its cocoon and become a moth or miller. Or when the bees find it burrowing among their brood, if they are numerous and thrifty, they will cut the combs away around it and get it out, and drop it on the bottom board, or fly clear away with it, as they cannot kill them by stinging. Bee-keepers now notice many worms, as the warmth from the advancing season and the increased number of bees now in the hive are developing them, and apply to me to transfer them to a new hive to get rid of the worms.

I do not at this time go to the pains of instructing them that I consider this a good omen, as boils on a man indicate constitutional vigor. They are cleaning their combs. By the time I get them transferred to a movable comb hive, where, as a general thing, they should be, they see that their combs are about clear of worms. If the bees are scarce in a hive, the worms will collect into a mass and build webs. If the bees can muster strength enough, they will cut the combs away all around the web and drag them out. Combs may often be found with holes and scars made in them in this way; but if the bees are not able to get them out, they will accumulate rapidly, soon consuming all the combs, and fill the hive with webs and cocoons, while large fat worms will even imbed themselves in the solid wood, so that I am frequently told : "You never saw such a mass of webs and worms as there was in one of my hives." Whilst the fact is I have seen them a great number of times, yet never relished the sight much.

If when the worms begin to mask their forces in a hive, the combs containing them could be taken out and cleaned every few days, until the bees could get the mastery of them, they could be saved, otherwise drive the bees out and take the honey. I have seldom derived much good from such stocks.

Good bee men tell me that they have suffered but very little loss from worms since they have changed to Italian bees.

When the bees are rid of the worms from the eggs of the previous year's raising, there will be but little more trouble again until after the swarming time, and hives that lose queens, or are weakened by over-swarming, are in danger from the great number of moths that will be prowling about at that time. Destroy all the worms and moths you can in the early part of the season, to prevent their breeding. Split alders laid under the hive offer a nice place for them to collect under where they can be destroyed. In my first attempts at harrowing I annoyed and worried myself exceedingly in holding the harrow to make it track right, and then did bungling work—the harrow going much as it pleased. I afterwards learned that my business was to guide the horses, and the harrow would come right of itself. And so with my bees. If they are kept right in other respects, I know there will be no danger from worms. I never lose any from this cause, neither do I direct much attention specially to their protection. The dread of the moth and a want of knowledge among bee-keepers, have given a fine chance to moth-proof bee-hive peddlers to operate. Doubtless most of them are honest in representing that they have just the hive that is needed. But when the keeper has tried the "never-fail" hive he finds that it too is subject to fail like all others. When I commenced selling hives, I had perhaps as complete a moth trap as is made, attached to my hive, in order to satisfy this anxiety for such arrangements, but afterwards concluded to make nothing to it but what was actually needed. I have not seen, nor do I expect to see, a moth-proof hive. Yet it is best to have hives made with few openings or cracks in them, that bees cannot enter to clean out the worms. I have seen entrances made to hives that bees could pass out and in at, but moths could not enter. I have seen a magnet placed at the entrance to paralyze the moth as it entered, but not to affect the bee. Some use pulverized glass or coarse sand glued to the boards about the entrance, presuming that bees can pass over such a rough surface and moths can not. A glass tube for an entrance, and various other contrivances to deceive the moth and lead it into a trap.

As ingenious a contrivance as I have seen is a piece of perforated tin to slide down over the entrance at night, and still give the bees air. [The moth does all its mischief at night]. The hives are all set along in a row, and a rod

passing along in front is attached to all the shutters. This
arrangement is connected by a lever to the hen-roost, so that
when tho fowls go to roost it closes all the hives, and when
they fly off in the morning it opens them. An objection to
this arrangement is, that on cloudy evenings they go to roost
too soon and shut out many of the bees. At other times a
lazy old hen would keep them in entirely too late.

PRUNING COMBS.

Is pruning ever necessary? If so, how often?

There is a common impression that bees somehow dislike
old dark combs, that worms will breed more in them and
that they cannot prosper long in such; hence the practice of
breaking out the combs frequently to have them replaced
with new ones. I have never yet seen anything to lead me
to believe that bees have any preference for new white combs
over old dark ones. However we may fancy the appearance
of white combs, and prefer to have our table honey stored in
it, there seems to be no reason for believing that one is not
as good for the bees as the other.

The only way in which it would seem they could be inju-
riously affected by old combs, is by the cells becoming so
small as to breed small bees. As every young bee that
hatches leaves a sheath or cocoon inside of its cell, if ten
young bees are hatched from each cell every season for ten
years it will contain one hundred cocoons, which one would
naturally suppose would make it very small.

It is true they do become some smaller; yet I am not able
to say that bees are more prosperous in new than in old
combs. I have seen bees that were very prosperous in combs
that were thirty years old. It would take close observation
to distinguish between the bees of such a hive and those of
one containing new combs. However, it may be best to
break out the part of the combs that are devoted to rearing
brood most every ten or twelve years.

As it costs bees a good deal to make comb, save it as long
as possible. The means and energy expended by bees
in making combs detract from the amount of honey and bees
produced. Colonies that expend much of these energies in
producing bees cannot yield so much honey or combs; nor if
they spend themselves in making combs and storing honey

can they rear so many bees. What resources are spent in one direction prevent their expenditure in another. One person will remark: "My bees did but little good last season ; they swarmed a good deal, but made but little honey." Another says: "Mine made me a great deal of honey, but yielded no swarms." If one of my hives yields me a great deal of honey, and another gives me several swarms, I do not object, but give them credit for being alike good.

WHEN TO PRUNE.

To break out the combs containing young bees, especially in the spring of the year, would be reckless waste. They could be broken out in November after breeding is over, but this is objectionable, because the combs broken out are just what is wanted by the bees to hover in during winter. It could be done a little better in March, but the bees still need it to hover in, besides there would still be considerable brood in the combs that should be broken out, and you must not dare to waste so essential a part of the colony at this time of year.

The only remaining time in the year that will do, is twenty-one days after the hive has given off a swarm. Every thing considered, this seems to be the best time. The young bees will then be all hatched out of the combs, except perhaps some drones; and it is no loss if some of these are destroyed, and there will be but few if any fresh eggs laid by the new queen.

HOW TO PROCEED.

Blow some smoke under the hive to subdue the bees. Invert the hive. Blow more smoke among the bees to drive them down off the combs that are to be taken out. Then proceed to cut or break out those parts of the combs that have been occupied by young bees. The rest of the combs in the bottom, as the hive now stands, and a little at the sides being filled with honey need not be touched. If the bees are too numerous to admit of getting the combs out whilst they are in when the hive is inverted, set an empty one on it and tie a sheet around where the hives meet, if you are afraid they will get out and sting you (although there is less danger of being stung now than there is at other seasons of the year); with a light hammer rap on the hive and the bees will all in a few minutes enter the upper hive. Now set the hive with the bees on the usual stand, and proceed to get out the old combs. The bees may then be run back into their hive as in hiving a swarm, or invert the hive containing the bees and set the one they had been in on top of it, and leave them standing thus until the next morning; against this time the bees will have all gone into the upper hive.

REMOVING DRONE COMBS.

It is often advisable to break out a portion of the drone combs when a colony produces too many drones. From a great many of my hives all the drone combs have been removed. It is poor economy to have a colony rearing a great horde of drones to eat honey instead of workers to make it, since a half dozen hives may raise enough for a whole neighborhood, and we know of no use for them except as a male bee, except it would be a few in each hive for the sake of company. When drone combs are broken out they frequently build the same kind in their place. If a movable comb hive be used when such a comb is taken out, a piece of empty worker comb may be fitted in its stead. In this way a hive can forever after be prevented from rearing drones, as they will have no cells suitable for rearing them in. Small or medium sized hives have much less drone combs than large ones.

TOOLS FOR CUTTING COMBS.

Two tools for cutting combs can be made by any blacksmith. They are convenient for cutting combs out of hives or honey out of honey boxes. To make a tool for cutting down the sides of the hive, take a three-eighths inch rod of steel, two feet long. Bend about two inches of the end of this at right angles, making a thin blade, both edges sharp, the side to go next to the hive flat, the other side beveled; this tool may be called the verticle.

Another tool, called the horizontal, is made in the same manner, except that the blade is made to lie flat on the bottom when you are cutting the combs out of an inverted hive. Have the under side flat and the top beveled; this blade need not be more than a fourth of an inch wide. This is used for cutting the combs loose from the lid or any place where they are to be cut horizontally. With these tools all the combs and honey can be taken from a hive without destroying the hive.

WAX.

Beeswax is made by putting the combs in a coffee sack or other strong loosely woven fabric, inserted in a kettle of boiling water. While boiling keep pressing and working it until all the wax comes through the bag. Then remove it. When the water cools the wax will be in a cake on the surface. To melt this wax over again once or twice in clean water purifies and whitens it. It is bleached by being laid in thin flakes in the sun.

RENDERING HONEY.

Honey may be rendered by mashing it up and placing it in a bag hung where it will be warm and drip from it into a vessel, or mash it up in a colander placed over a vessel in a warm oven. Some of the wax that will melt and run through can be skimmed off when the honey cools. Put the refuse combs into the honey boxes for the bees to empty. Persons who have much honey and wish to empty it out of the combs in order to have them refilled, can obtain a patent machine for that purpose by applying to S. Wagoner, Washington, D. C.

THE APIARY.

The bees should be near the house where they can be heard when they swarm. They should also be where they would not feel the north and west wind, where they can have a calm warm place to light. It makes but little difference which way the hives face; perhaps an easterly or southeasterly exposure is best. It is well if they can have the sun two or three hours in the morning, and as many in the evening, but shaded during the heat of the day. The shade of a tree or vine is good to break the heat of the sun, and keeps the combs from melting. A hedge, a high board fence, or building on the north and west are a protection against the strong winds which destroy very many laboring bees in the spring, when one bee is worth as much as a dozen in the latter part of summer, as they are much needed at this time of year to take care of the brood and keep it warm.

If in April the day has been rather warm and the evening cool and windy, hundreds of bees may be found on the ground in front of the hive perhaps loaded with bee-bread, but exhausted from the flight and chilled with the cold. As they approach the hive they relax their exertions and a slight whiff of wind dashes them on the ground from which they are unable to arise again. And before the sun warms them the next morning they will be dead. For this reason I prefer having my bees near the ground so that if any drop and cannot fly again, they may crawl into the hive. Were it not that in dashing rains the water splashes up and wets the hive, I would prefer having my hives within two or three inches of the ground. As it is, I usually set them from six to twelve inches up, and lean a short board from the ground to the entrance of the hive, that bees may crawl up when they cannot fly. Hives placed near the ground if upset from any cause are less likely to be injured, as Bunyan says: "He that is down need fear no fall."

THE STAND.

For a stand for a hive lay down two pieces of scantling. If it is desired to have it higher lay two others across these ; lay a short board on these. If any one wishes to expend something more on a stand they can make one more beautiful but I doubt if it be any better.

A good cheap stand for a box hive is made by using a board as wide as the hive, and cut long enough to extend six or eight inches in front for an alighting board for the bees. Nail down through this into strips two or three inches thick to keep the board from warping, and to raise it off the ground where no stand is used.

KEEP HIVES SEPARATE.

For different reasons it is preferable to have each hive on a separate stand, instead of the common practice of setting several on one board. When a number of hives are on one board the bees are much inclined to run together to their great disadvantage, besides they are more likely to be crowded together. It is not good to have them closer than three or four feet apart. I would prefer where there is room to separate them ten feet. Persons sometimes tell me they have seen bee-keepers who would set their bees down on the ground, here and there and everywhere, apparently giving them no attention, and had more luck than those who built fine houses for them and went to great expense. I do not doubt it. They blundered on some good rules, but had they observed the same rules intentionally they would not have fared worse. Bee-houses will break the storm and keep the hives dry, in other respects they are a disadvantage.

HOW BEES KNOW THEIR HOME.

Bees are not attracted to their home by instinct as by a magnet, but are governed by their senses in marking their locality. In early spring a large portion of the bees that fly out are young ones that have never been out, and the old ones having been confined to the hive by winter, seem to have forgotten their situation. Consequently when they fly out in the spring they do not leave the hive in a straight line, but only go a few inches, then with their heads to the hive, and oscillate back and forth in front of it; then move farther back, still hovering in front of the hive with their heads always towards the entrance, occasionally advancing towards it, as if to note more particularly the exact place of entrance. Then after making a few larger circles in the air, they start in a straight line for the distance. On returning they come directly to the hive and enter. The surrounding objects and the color of the hive seem to be noted by the bees. After bees have got their course in the spring, should the hive be moved two or three rods, they in flying out will not note the place; but if they are in clear open ground, they will generally find their place on returning. But should other objects intervene, or hives be sitting close by, it would be quite certain that a great number of them would be lost if the hive be moved more than two or three feet from their old stand. They would either wander about until they would die, or they would attempt to enter another hive and be killed. If I wish to move a hive a few rods after the bees have their course, I move them two or three feet each day, until I get them from among other hives. Then move them three or four feet each day, thus tolling them along until I get them where I want them. When they have been moved a short distance the search seems to make them note the new position of their home.

WHEN MOVED A DISTANCE.

The result is different when the hive has been moved a mile and a half or more; they note the new locality and all return to it. If the hive is closed and shook or rapped on, or the bees smoked to alarm them when moving them a short distance, they are much more likely to note the new locality when they come out.

HIVES CLOSE TOGETHER.

From the foregoing facts may be seen some of the disadvantages of having hives of uniform size, shape and color sitting close together, especially when there are any operations to be performed requiring any change of the position of hives. It can be seen, too, how if two hives in the same yard are to be united, if it is desired to save all the bees, they should be first brought together gradually.

A QUEEN MAY MISS ITS HIVE.

Another serious disadvantage from having hives sitting close together is, that the queen in going out on her hymeneal excursions, and returning to the hive may make the ludicrous mistake of entering a neighboring hive and being killed, which at this time would prove fatal to her colony as they would have no brood to rear another.

THE COVER OF THE HIVE.

A cheap cover is as good as any, so it keeps off the rain and the sun. A wide board, three feet long, with strips nailed across it to prevent warping, will do very well. A roof shaped cover made of two boards, using triangular shaped boards at the ends, on the under side, to nail to, is a good plan. Those who think they must have bee-houses can devise them to suit their fancy. Some make them with tiers one above another on both sides of a room, leaving a walk between them, and have it convenient for shutting up for winter. But for most bee-keepers they will not pay expenses.

A JOURNAL.

Use a pocket memorandum book for a bee-journal. Have each bee-hive numbered. It would be convenient to have labels of tin or wood with numbers on them to be tacked on the hives. Have a page in the journal corresponding with the number of each hive, in which may be recorded the condition of the hive at any time: when it was hived—when it gave off a swarm, and how often—how much surplus honey it furnished—whether it was strong or weak, etc. Such a book is convenient for reference.

LUCK AND NOTIONS.

Some tell us "they will buy a hive of bees and see what sort of *luck* they will have." Others "somehow never could have any *luck*, and so gave their bees into their wives' care to see if they would do any better." I have known such experiments to work well. There is a common opinion that "if a person sells bees they will sell their luck." (There *is* danger of this if he always sells his best.) Others will not give them away for the same reason.

Some, to make the thing entirely sure, will neither sell or give away, but will allow one to come and steal one away, leaving some money instead of it on the stand, and afterwards conclude from the smallness of the amount of money left that perhaps this plan is no better than either of the others. To trade sheep for bees is considered more favorable to success. "When a member of the family dies, you must go and whisper it to the bees, or they will do no good afterwards." "When the owner dies they will dwindle to nothing." I can certify to this being sometimes the case.

It is supposed to be necessary to "go to the bees at midnight of New Year's, and tell the bees that the old year is gone." (I have a good deal of confidence in the success of persons who will give them such care.) "It is bad luck to quarrel about bees." "Bees will do no good during war." This seemed very evident during the two first years of our war. However, my faith in this saying was much weakened when I learned that they were doing excellently in the Western States, but perhaps they had not received the intelligence there, as it seems they did very poorly there during the latter part of the war. "I never saw a king bee." "They will do no good in the valley." "They will do no good on the hills." A boy coming to my house, hastened to tell me that "my bees were going off; I saw two or three going past the barn." A man stopped in at nine o'clock at night to tell me that he thought my bees were swarming, as he heard them making a great noise as he came past. A boy in the city asked me how I got so many bees in my hive: "Did you catch them on the flowers and put them there." A neighbor woman who had just got a hive of bees, took me to them about the time that drones began to appear, to show me some strange bees that were entering her hive; she said they were much larger than her bees; she supposed they were mine. A neighbor of an acquaintance of mine called on him to get an Italian drone to put in his hive of native bees, as he wished to improve his stock. He said "he knew it would have the desired effect, as queens were fond of strange company." They did very well afterwards.

A prominent school-teacher's wife asked me if I could make bees? To which I honestly replied that I could not. "Well," says she, "I did not know—they used to make them over the mountains out of bees-wax, or something of that kind, and put them in the sun to hatch."

The most of the foregoing proverbs are attributed modestly to "It-is-said," who is a roving character, who, when you go to ask him the reasons for his sayings, cannot be found.

Exaggerated tales and imaginary theories about bees are numerous. The amount of foolish or crude notions about them suggests to me that bee-keeping has been behind the times. Yet there is a generosity manifested by men in dealing about bees that is not so much shown when dealing with other stock. (I do not now speak of those who make it their exclusive business.) It affords me pleasure to discern so noble a streak in human nature. They only keep bees for the use of their families and their friends. Many seem glad to give away all the honey they do not actually need. It is common to give a swarm of bees to those who wish to make a start, or to tell them to take a hive, and if they do well they may give them a swarm some time. Men generally do not value bees for the money that is in them, but as they do a choice horse, or other favorite animal. They love to sit or lie beside to hear and watch them. There is something there that charms.

Why do not females engage in bee-culture? They can manage it as well as males. I know some that are making a good business out of it. This would add another to the variety of female employments, which will tend to enhance their wages.

TRANSPORTATION.

I have assisted in preparing bees for shipment to California, and have sent hives of bees to the different States, and moved a great many a short distance by rail road and by private conveyance, and know that with proper care bees can be shipped most any distance, and know also that with bad care they can be destroyed in a very short journey. Two things are to be guarded against—smothering and breaking of combs.

Bees should not be moved in hot weather. Spring is a better time than fall, as the combs are not so likely to be broken from the weight of honey. The older the combs the less likely they are to break. If the weather is very cold stir the bees up an hour or two before starting to haul them. In very cold weather the combs are quite brittle. The excitement among the bees caused by shaking them will generate heat in the hive and make the combs tough.

Carry them on a spring wagon, a sled, or the cars. Invert the hive, tie or tack a thin cloth over the mouth of it, and haul it bottom up in order that the weight of the honey may rest on the lid of the hive. Combs are not nearly so likely to break if the hive is inverted. If the combs are broken in hauling, leave the hive inverted until the combs are united by the bees. If the combs are fallen out of place,

straighten them and put wads of paper between them to hold
them in place. The cloth over the mouth of the hive will
give the bees air enough. Hauling bees a half hour or more
generally removes the disposition to sting. Set the bees on
the stand where you intend them to remain before letting
them fly.

A convenient arrangement for carrying a swarm is a tea
chest with wire cloth over the mouth or bottom of it, and also
over a hole three or four inches square made in the side of it.
Have a leather handle tacked on the top. One of such hives
can be carried in each hand conveniently. To secure the
wire cloth to the bottom, use a light wooden frame or strips
tacked all around the edge of the wire cloth, with inch and
a half screws through them to fasten to the bottom of the
box. If only screwed two-thirds way in they will hold the
box up so as to give the bees air when the box is set down.

SWARMING.

It is said, "A swarm of bees in May is worth a ton of hay;
a swarm of bees in June is worth a silver spoon ; but a swarm
of bees in July is not worth a fly."

If this be so the number of swarms not worth a fly are
many more than those worth a ton of hay. The last half of
June yields the greatest number of swarms. The latter part
of every season is not alike good for making honey, and some
years a colony will collect as much after the first of July as
they will other years after the first of June. Yet it is true
that swarms in July are generally of little value in this locality. One in the middle of May is worth as much as a half
dozen the first of July. A variety of circumstances combine
to make one hive give off several swarms, and another apparently as good, not any.

That bees come out of their hives in swarms, make a great
noise, then settle and wait awhile where the keeper can hive
them, is a phenomenon admirably adapted to the wants of
bee-culturists. The fact that a colony of bees will not produce nearly so much honey if they give off a swarm as if they
did not, has induced some to adopt the non-swarming system,
which besides being less trouble has some other advantages,
but the advantages of the increase of stock in the swarming
plan far exceed them. As the capacity of a queen's laying

is not much above what takes place in an ordinary hive, the idea of producing a monster colony to fill a large bee-house or a garret is preposterous. It is true there have been cases of an extraordinary yield of honey and combs, but they seldom double the number of bees contained in a medium sized hive, and will not in this region yield fifty pounds of honey. Such a hive if kept twelve years would not yield over five hundred pounds of honey. Whilst one colony on the swarming plan by doubling their numbers only every two years, would at the end of twelve years have produced sixty-four swarms, which would then in one season, at twenty pounds each yield more than a thousand pounds of honey.

WHEN TO EXPECT SWARMS.

There is no probability that a colony will swarm except it is collecting honey quite freely. They would be reckless to start a new colony when there was no probability that it could be maintained. If the hive is very large so that the bees are not likely to fill it, or if they should fill it, if it contains three or four bushels, there will not likely be more than one chance in ten for their swarming. But if they are gathering honey freely and are strong in numbers so as to be crowded for room, and the weather is fair, swarms may be expected to issue between nine in the morning and three in the afternoon. There is some variation from this rule, especially in after-swarms. About the time that swarms are expected, invert the hive and blow a little smoke among the bees to drive them off the combs. If queen-cells are found capped over, a swarm may be looked for immediately. Although if all the circumstances are favorable, they will sometimes swarm when they have got no farther on at most than to have queen cells started. This was generally the case last season.

Drones generally begin to appear before the swarming commences. But the presence of capped queen cells is the best evidence of their intentions to swarm. To the inexperienced this turning up a hive to examine it is quite a formidable undertaking, but the dread of it soon vanishes on trial. In all operations involving danger of an onset, be sure to always have the first blow. Give them smoke enough to alarm them and make them submissive before the hive is

moved in the least; if the bees 'are on the outside smoke
them in.   If the bees have their queen cells capped and all
preparations ready for swarming, a sudden change to wet and
stormy weather will keep them in for several days.   They
may then swarm even if the weather is unfavorable.   But
if the weather continues bad, or the yield of honey begins to
diminish, they may destroy their queen cells and not swarm
that season.   Even if a colony is ready to swarm, a sudden
failure in the honey resources may make them give up
swarming for the season, and sometimes when it has not this
effect it would have been better for them if it had.

The failure of honey-gathering also has the same effect on
their rearing of drones, as was plainly manifested when the
June frost of 1859 destroyed the bloom and seemed to give
the bees the impression that winter was set in.   They immediately commenced killing their drones.   Even the drone
brood was torn out of the cells and tumbled out of the hives.
In a few days the clover was yielding honey again as freely
as ever.   They reared a new set of drones and swarmed.
The destruction of drones at any time may be taken as evidence that swarming is over for the present, and that there
is not much honey-gathering.   If swarming is kept back for
several days by bad weather, a number of colonies may issue
the same day.   So have plenty of hives on hand, and keep
a look out the first fair day that occurs, if all the other circumstances for swarming are favorable.   In the morning of
a day in which a colony intends giving off a swarm, the bees
are generally hanging about the entrance and are very quiet.
But few bees fly out and in, especially for an hour before
they swarm.   From ten to thirty minutes before swarming,
whilst they are yet still on the outside, there is a great agitation inside, running to and fro and filling themselves with
honey.   I know of no reliable sign of swarming other than
those I have mentioned.   Some say they can always tell
when a colony is going to swarm by hearing the piping of the
queens, but this is speaking rather fast.   It never takes place
before first swarms.*

This peculiar piping, which is different from any other noise
made by the bees, and sounds like pronouncing the word
peep, is occasioned by the contention of a plurality of queens,

* By first, or top swarms, I mean the first swarm that each colony gives off in the
season.   The second, third, &c., are called after-swarms or casts.

which of course do not exist at first swarming. If any one doubts whether the old queen leaves with the first swarm, all he has to do to convince himself of the fact, if he has a movable comb hive, is to open it after they have swarmed, and he will never be able to find a hatched queen in the hive. The absence of eggs in the hive from four to fifteen days or more after the swarm has left is evidence that there is no queen there to lay them.

One man tells me he cropped the wing of a young queen when hiving a swarm. The next season the bees forced this cropped winged queen out with the swarm. He supposed they had some antipathy towards her, and he was provoked at his bees, that for five years in succession they forced out this cropped winged queen with the top swarm. Another Virginia bee-keeper is sure he can convince me that it is not the old but a young queen that leaves with the swarm, by the fact that he cropped the wing of a queen that had dropped on the ground in swarming, and then put her with the swarm. The next season he watched this swarm closely, and the queen that came off with the first swarm was a young one with perfect wings. "How could I overthrow that argument?" I remarked, "that all queens die sometime. The fact that his queen dropped on the ground last season was evidence that she was then old."

It is said that when a queen begins to manifest infirmness, the bees to prevent the danger of her dying and leaving them without eggs or queen, start young ones and then destroy the old one. This is most probably true. But be this as it may, all queens die within from three to five years, or at most six, and new queens are reared.

This Virginian's cropped queen had died. They had reared another, and she, the eldest one, and the only one in the hive, came with the swarm.

Some feel sure it is the old queen leaves with the first swarms, as they have often noticed them so imperfect that they dropped down and could not fly. I can easily imagine how a decrepit old queen, burdened with thousands of eggs would be equally as clumsy as the young unfertilized one. The Virginian to whom I have referred, also attempted to prove to me that bees live for several years, by the fact that a swarm of bees had been clustered where he could not remove them all at once, and removing them by passing a long bladed sharp knife several times through the cluster, he cut the legs and wings off a great many of the bees. Three years afterwards he found many of these same crippled bees. I had nothing to say, only that ho had a great deal more skill than I had in identifying individual bees after so long a time.

But to return to the bees about to swarm. Many tell us the queen comes out and all tbe bees follow her. So also in clustering, and when sho enters a hive they all rush in with delight. I never find it so with my bees. Although tho bees seem aware of the necessity of her presence among them, and are slow to settle without her, nor will they remain clustered or stay in the hive except she be with them. Casts or after-swarms, have young unfertile queens which are not so steady in their habits as old ones, and do not settle so readily with the swarm, and are more likely to come out after being hived. But in first swarms I never see tho queen until a great many and generally nearly all the swarm has issued. How they decide what bees will come out, and what ones will stay in, I cannot tell. I am glad we have not to comprehend every thing; and this, like most every thing else, will como right independent of our knowing how. Generally nearly three-fourths of the bees leave with the swarm, old and young, but principally the old. [An old bee is known by the ends of its wings being worn ragged, also the yellow down is more or less worn off their bodies, giving them a darker appearance than young ones.] The bees have now rushed out precipitously and are whizzing in every direction, making as much noise as the hundred hives at work close by. Who could help admiring so beautiful a phenomenon as the swarming of bees, especially when there is added to this the rustic music of horns and tin pans. It is pleasing to bear such things on account of their expression of the feeling of enthusiasm and tho associations of early times. Besides it pleases the children, and so far as I c in see is no hindrance to the clustering of the bees. It is well if there are no high trees for tbem to cluster on. It is best to make no delay in biving them, for if left too long they may leave and go to tbe woods. If you have many bees, and especially if a few days previous has been bad weather, there is danger that other swarms may issuo and settle with them. If a swarm is coming out whilst anotber is yet unbived, throw a sheet over the first and tie it in, that the second cannot get at it. No difference how many come out in such a case, they will all light together. If whilst you are hiving a swarm there is a likelihood that another will issue before you are done, go to all your hives and examine them hastily. If there is the agitation in the hive that is preparatory to swarming, sprinkle those outside with water, and they will go in and retard swarming for a half hour or more. If two or more large swarms go together, they should always bo divided. To do this you must have some knowledge and a good deal of patience. Put an equal number of the bees into two hives, watching as they enter for a queen. If you find her, place her under a tumbler or in a wire cage.* If you do not see her you may have a queen in each hive; if not, the one that is queenless will soon manifest it by running rapidly about the entrance, showing much uneasiness. Set this hive now on a sheet and tie it so that the bees will not get out, and lay it on its side to keep them from smothering, while you shake the bees out of the other hive and run them in again until you find a queen. Put her in your queenless hive, and you are done. If you find a queen when first hiving them, set the hives on their stands and when one of them begins to show signs of queenlessness, give it the caged queen. When hiving, it is generally convenient to use a table-cloth or newspaper laid on the table or the ground. Set the hive on this, raising one side of it a little to let the bees enter. If it is desired to look for the queen, shake the bees down, one, two or three feet from the hive, so as to afford a better opportunity to look for her as they pass in. Her slightly yellowish color, her long legs and body, her more majestic movements among her people, are likely to attract the eye. Do not be expecting to find her among the thick clusters of bees ; she is no more likely to be there than any other bee,† nor do the bees pay any regard to her in these states of excitement, except that it is necessary for her to be somewhere among them. If she does not come out of the hive, or if she drops on the ground, when they swarm,

---

* To make a cage, take a piece of wire cloth three inches square, twelve to sixteen meshes to the inch. Bend this around a flat stick so as to make a flat tube, and put a plug of paper in each end.

† If a queen gets into a swarm to which she does not belong (as is the case occasionally with queens of two swarms that have gone together), the bees will confine her, by clustering in a ball the size of a hen's egg, or move so tightly around her that you may toss them in your hand like a ball. To get her from among them without injury, throw them all into water and they will let her go.

3*

the bees, after flying awhile, will return to the hive. If they
have clustered and she is taken from them they will all go back
to their hive. If they have been hived and lose their queen
in any way within a day or two, before they have become
well established in their new abode, they will all come out and
go to their old home. These facts have given the impression
that if the queen be taken from a colony the bees will all
leave. But in no case that I know of, except those that I have
mentioned, will the loss of the queen have such an effect.
Even a dead queen given to a swarm will ordinarily induce
the bees to stay. But I do not know that her presence would
have any other effect.

When colonies are well established in their hives and disposed to swarm out at improper times, I have often taken
their queen from them to induce them to stay. As there is
no likelihood of their swarming if they have no queen to go
with them, when a branch containing the bees can be cut,
it is best to set the hive on its stand and carry the swarm to
it to be hived. I usually take a pint or two of bees on my
hand and empty them at the entrance of the hive first. A
ladle or pan can be used for this purpose, if one does not like
to use his hand, but there is comparatively little danger of
being stung at this time, as they generally fill themselves with
honey before leaving the parent hive ; and bees filled with
any thing sweet rarely sting. When the bees have been
placed at the entrance of the hive, some of them will enter,
and being joyed at discovering what seems to them the home
they need, they will get up a general hum, and those outside,
attracted by the sound, will hasten in, buzzing as they go.
Then shake down the rest of the swarm, and they will all go
in ; if they are inclined to take wing, a little water sprinkled
on them will prevent it. If they are slow to enter, gently
shake the cloth or paper they are on, or brush them with a
quill to hurry them. Be sure to get them all in before you
leave them, as the queen may not be in, and eventually, she
may take wing and the whole swarm go to the woods. So
soon as all are in that can be got in conveniently, set the
hive where·it is intended to remain. Those that are still flying about will return to the parent stock. But if they are
left sitting where they are hived until night, and then
removed, a great number of the bees will have marked their
locality, like a colony in the spring of the year, and when

they fly out the next day will come back to their first stand, and be lost instead of returning to their old home. Shade the hive well, at least for a few days. If water is thrown on the hive occasionally, the evaporation from the hive will cool it and make it agreeable.

A gentleman who had agreed to furnish his first swarm to his neighbor had another to come out at the same time and settle with it, he disliked to sell them both for the price of one, so he ran them both into a large hive and left them sitting in the sun, whilst he came eight miles for me to divide them. When he returned, the bees had become overheated and had left for—he knew not where. If a swarm begins to return to the hive without clustering, the old hive might be set away or closed, and a new one set on its stand for them to enter. Look on the ground for the queen (which has most likely dropped down) and put her with them. When the bees commence clustering in some undesirable place, I take a handful of leafy branches and hold them in my hand immediately over the cluster. I have sometimes used a clump of dead mullen tops tied together to resemble a swarm of bees, to have the swarm settle on it. As they are all the time inclined to work upwards in clustering, take a handful or two gently from the cluster and place them on the swarming bush in your hand to form a nucleus to which the rest will be inclined to unite. Then stir the bees below with a quill or branch, or what is less likely to anger them, a little smoke held immediately under them will make them move; when on the bush they can be carried to the hive. If a few are inclined to cluster on the branch after the main portion of the swarm has been removed, they could be collected in this way and taken to the hive; or hold the branch to one side, or shake it until the bees are attracted by the sound in the hive and enter it. To place a smoking rag on the place where bees persist in clustering, or rub the parts with catnip, wormwood, or other bitter herbs, will make them less inclined to light there. They will sometimes persist in clustering where the queen has been. A lady, at a fair where I was playing with a colony of bees, was standing near, my queen got out of her cage and lit on her shoulder and the bees commenced clustering with her, and it was with difficulty that she could prevent them from lighting there, even after the queen had been removed. A hive or box is sometimes set immediately over the bees, and they run up into it. When high up on a branch, a large basket could be fastened to a pole, and reaching up, jar the bees into it; let the basket down gently, and cover the basket over with a cloth until the bees have become quiet, they can then be hived. Nothing is needed in the hive to induce the bees to stay, except to be cool, clean and rather rough where the bees have to fasten their combs. To rub the hive inside with peach tree leaves, with hickory leaves, or salt water, or sugar water is all unnecessary. I use none of these and could hardly have better luck than I have. Some persons lose one-fourth of their bees by their going to the woods either before or after they were hived. I have not had one hive in one hundred to leave me when I have been at home to attend to them. Although I consider this rather remarkable, yet am strongly inclined to think that the proper management of swarms has something to do with it.

DO BEES HAVE THEIR HOME IN THE WOODS SELECTED BEFORE LEAVING THE HIVE?

This is an unsettled question, yet it seems most probable that some of them do, at least when they come out of the hive and go immediately in a straight line to the tree.

BEE TREES.

In swarming time bees are often found clearing the hollow of a tree, and soon after a swarm has been known to enter it. When bees are hunting a home they can be seen hovering about a hole in a tree, and flying up and down and around it apparently in search of something; whilst if a colony already lodged in a tree, the bees will be flying to and from it more in a straight line. Observance of this rule would prevent many a large tree from being unnecessarily cut for bees in swarming time.

TO CUT A BEE TREE.

Cut a bee tree as soon as a swarm has been known to enter, before the bees commence building combs, otherwise defer it until the bees are just commencing to make honey the next spring. The combs will then be stronger and being well emptied of honey, will be less likely to break and drown the bees in honey. Besides, if a colony is put into a hive, they can maintain themselves and fill the hive. If the bees are put in a movable comb hive, all the brood and nicest of the combs can be fitted into it, so as to give them a good start. (See transferring). Besides, if their queen is killed they can rear another. If the bees are in a good tree it is best to go in partnership with the owner in cutting it. When there were no bees in this county more than two miles west of Cadiz, a swarm of them came to a man at Cassville, seven miles west, so they must have gone five miles or more.

CASTS OR AFTER-SWARMS.

Medium or small sized hives yield swarms sooner than large ones. They are also more likely to give off after-swarms. After the first swarm leaves, there is a thousand or more hatching every day, so that in a few days the hive will have become quite populous again. They will have several young queens hatching, generally about ten days after the first swarm, so that if the weather is favorable and the honey resources abundant there will be a likelihood of another swarm issuing. I suppose there are more second swarms come off on the tenth day than on any other, and nine-tenths of them will come between the eighth and twelfth days. Sometimes they will come earlier than the eighth day, and others may run even as far as the fifteenth. But after the seventeenth day, no more swarms need be looked for that season, as all the young queens will be hatched out. If the bees are not gathering honey pretty freely, you need not look for swarms, no difference how much they lie out. Do not be looking for swarms all fall, nor complaining of the bees because " they are lying out and doing no good ;" it is not their fault. If there was plenty of honey in the flowers you could hardly keep them from gathering it If young queens are found dead at the entrance of the hive after the first swarm leaves, it is pretty sure evidence that they have given up swarming any more. When they design swarming again it seems they guard the queens in the cells, feeding them and keeping them in their cells so that they may not get out and destroy each other as they are certain to do if left to their own way. They thus keep them until they need them for whatever swarms they see proper to give off. I have had eight or ten queens hatched in my hand in fifteen minutes by taking the cells out of a hive so the bees could not confine them to the cells. So many young queens just hatching when the after-swarms are coming off is the reason that a number of queens come out with the after-swarms, and sometimes cause them to light in different places. But if hived they will all be killed against the next morning. If one queen is allowed to hatch in advance of others, she will proceed immediately to destroy them, by eating a hole in the side of the cells and stinging the young queens. A cell that has been torn open by the violence of a queen may be known by its having a hole torn in the side. Where a queen has hatched naturally the opening is in the end. In rearing Italian queens I have always to be sure not to let the young queens remain in the hive or nucleus a single day beyond their time of hatching, as all but one are sure to be destroyed. If any of those bee-keepers who keep several queens running at large in the hive for any length of time, will inform me how I can do so I will compensate them well for the information, as it will be of great service to me. The presence of so many queens often occasions a great deal of annoyance, by inducing the giving off more swarms than are capable of taking care of themselves, and the mother colony is so reduced that it has not bees enough to make any surplus honey nor to cover its combs to guard against worms and robbers. For if they keep on swarming until the sixteenth day, nearly all the hatched bees will go out and there will only be the brood of four or five days' laying of the old queen to hatch, and it will be a full month before the brood of the young queen can be hatching. It is not strange that such colonies should be taken by the worms in August when they are most abundant, and the bee-keeper will very naturally say: "There, the worms have destroyed my best colony." Or, perhaps, it is robbed by other bees, and the blame is charged to the robbers. Or, perhaps, the young queens of these after-swarms or of the mother colony in their flight to meet the drones may be lost. As they now have no brood in the hive from which to rear another, the colony will soon dwindle away and become a prey to worms and robbers. These evils may be very much remedied by destroying all the queen-cells in the old hive, except one after the first swarm. This prevents after-swarms. But when the box-hive is used it is not very convenient to get at all the cells. I therefore adopt what I consider in many respects a much superior plan; one that is practical, and that I hope to see largely put in practice. It is this : Have some young queens reared on the plan given for rearing Italian queens ; give one of these young queens to the old colony as soon as the swarm has left. They are then in good condition for receiving a strange queen, and she will generally proceed to destroy the embryo queens, thus preserving after-swarms. This queen will be laying eggs at the rate of perhaps one thousand per day, for eighteen or twenty days before a young queen of their own rearing could be laying, as it would be about ten days before she would hatch, and about ten more before she would be laying. In absence of a hatched queen, a queen in the cell nearly ready to hatch could be given them, which would generally prevent after-swarming. She would be hatched before many young bees would have emerged to make the hive throng. So they would not be much inclined to swarm and would let her destroy the embryos. A hive that has given off a swarm from six to ten days previous, would furnish the necessary nymphs. Or remove the queen from a colony a week or more before the time you expect swarms and it will produce the necessary cells. Queens in the cells will rarely be received any other way than kindly. A hatched queen that is not fertile, will not be received nearly so well as one that is already a mother. A fertile queen, even if she is a stranger in the hive will be clustered over by the bees and fed through the meshes of the wire cage, whilst an unfertilized queen will be noticed but little more than a worker. Such have always to take care of themselves until they become mothers. If the apiarian wishes to change his native bees to Italians or improve his Italians, he can do it very conveniently by supplying the queens or cells from his best Italian stock. Every thing considered, I think it best not to aim at more than one swarm from each old stock. Any one who thinks this is too slow a way of getting along let him calculate the product of five hives of bees, just doubling themselves each year for twelve years, allowing the surplus honey to pay the expenses. At the end of twelve years sell the whole stock at the rate of ten dollars each. I am not sure but he will conclude that a desire for a faster increase savors a little of avarice. I admit that after-swarms sometimes do well, and where all the circumstances are favorable they may be tolerated. But in four cases out of five, it is

better either to prevent after-swarms or run them back when
they swarm, or unite two or three of them to make them very
strong.   To prevent a swarm from issuing or to put it back
insures the safety of the old stock from all the effects of weak-
ness, and the honey that would have been made by the bees
in a new hive would be made in surplus boxes of the old one.
The united force of two or three small swarms will often
make one very good one, which nothing but experience seems
sufficient to convince most persons is worth more than three
or four poor ones.   Therefore, prevent after-swarming if you
can ; if not, put them back into the hive they came out of,
destroying the queen, if you can find her ; or put two or three
small swarms together.   If you can kill all the queens but
one, do so.   A swarm can generally bo run into another
several days after they have been hived.   It is often the case,
that a colony will destroy a few intruders to their hive ; while
a whole colony run in at once will overwhelm them, and they
receive them as their equals.   Should there be any show o
resistance, a few whiffs of tobacco-smoke among them wil[l]
generally restore peace.

   The plan I have just recommended, of supplying queens
or queen-cells, has these advantages : They prevent the apiarian the disadvantages of after-swarms where they are not
wanted.   From five to ten thousand more bees will be reared
by not having to wait for the development of queens in the
ordinary way.   And, what is certainly a matter of the highest
importance is, *the bee-keeper can always furnish queens bred
from his best stocks, whether they be native or Italian.* Somo few
stocks of bees seem prosperous from generation to generation,
producing most all the profits of the apiary ; while others, seem-
ingly with the same facilities, get nothing done.   Always breeding from the best producers, I am fully convinced will very materially improve the thrift of the apiary.   Some queens breed
but little ; to remove such and give them a good one is desirable.   From my own experience, also, I feel fully convinced
that during the first and second years of a queen's life sho is
more prolific than in the after part ; and it is an advantage
to replace the old queen with a young ono.   Keeping such a
journal as I have recommended, would be of great advantage
in the foregoing modo of management.

ARTIFICIAL SWARMING.

Any one who decides for his hens when they must set, must not be too fast in objecting to artificial swarms. I have for years practised artificial swarming about as much as the natural way and like each about alike. I love to see bees swarm in the usual way, and if they always come just when I want them and have time to attend to them, I would perhaps let them have their own way generally. But if they are likely to swarm when I expect to be from home, or so engaged that I cannot attend to them; or if they are near some high trees where it would be difficult to get them down, if they clustered on them; or if I desire turning all the strength of my bees to making swarms instead of surplus honey, I take the matter into my own hand, and divide them to suit myself: and it seems to make no more difference which of the ways than it does to a hen whether they are her own or another's eggs she sits on.

HOW TO PROCEED.

Go to a hive that can spare a swarm; blow smoke on the bees outside the hive to drive them in; blow a little in the under end of the hive to make the bees submissive; invert the hive; set an empty one on the top of it; tie a sheet around where the two hives meet to prevent the bees coming out; with a light hammer give the hive a few raps; the bees will proceed to fill themselves with honey, as they do when they swarm naturally; then in five minutes commence rapping briskly on the hive, and in ten or twenty minutes two-thirds or more of the bees will be in the upper hive. These, with those that will return from foraging, will constitute the new swarm. You need not be afraid to lean the top of the hive over some to see if there have enough bees gone up. They will not sting at this stage of progress. It is supposed that the queen has gone into the upper hive, and that the old one has the means of rearing others. Their relative condition is therefore much the same as if a swarm had been given off naturally, except the old hive will not have queen-cells so far on the way. But this makes no difference if you will only supply them with a queen-cell, as recommended elsewhere, which would now be of great advantage to do. While this operation is going on, an empty hive should be set on the stand of the old hive (this is called the decoy hive), to catch the bees that return from foraging. Now set the decoy hive to one side, and set the hive with the new swarm in its place on the stand of the old hive; then set the old hive away a rod or more; shake the bees out of the decoy hive in front of the new hive and they will enter it, and you are done. If you do not succeed in getting the queen in the new hive, you will know it in a few minutes by the bees coming out and manifesting much anxiety. If you have not got her you will have to drive again until you find her. As soon as they commence running up, I tilt the hive to one side and watch for her among them. The old hive will seem deserted for a few days, but the great number of bees hatching every day will soon replenish it. A good swarm of bees thus driven will weigh about five or six pounds.

ANOTHER PLAN.

If a hive cannot afford a swarm itself, it is a good plan to make one from two, thus: Drive all the bees out of one hive, call it No. 1; remove another strong one, which we will call No. 2, a rod or more from its stand. Now take No. 1, which has no bees, and set it where No. 2 stood, and two-thirds of the bees from No. 2 will enter it and rear a queen; but it is better to give them one. All hives that have to rear queens, whether they have given a swarm naturally, or otherwise, should be examined at the time the new queen should have brood and see if all is right. [See Loss of Queens.] But artificial swarms can be made much more conveniently by using movable comb hives. Open the hive from which you wish to take a swarm; look over the combs until you find the queen; lift out the comb with the queen and bees adhering; set this on the centre of the new hive on the stand of the old one, and set the old one away a rod or more. Three-fourths of the bees will leave and enter the new hive. If you have an empty comb in a frame to put in the old hive in place of the one taken out it would be a great advantage; if not, set all the combs in the hive together, so as to receive an empty frame at the outside; if you can now supply them with a queen or cell it will be a great help. Some fear that by artificial divisions there will not be the right proportion of honey-gatherers, wax-workers and nurses left in the hive. I do not know that there is such a division of labor, each having its appropriate work to perform. Any one can do all the parts, yet the young bees mainly do the nursing; these are the ones mostly left in the hive when it has been moved to a new locality to let the bees fly back to the old stand. If the bees and honey be equally distributed, the hive that is queenless will construct drone combs principally in the empty space in the hive until their young queen becomes fertile. So much drone comb will make the hive an unprofitable one afterwards. The hive that has all the brood and honey of course does not need so many bees as the one that has neither.

LOSS OF QUEENS.

Loss of queens is a fruitful source of loss of colonies. For if they have not the means to produce another queen they will inevitably dwindle to nothing. This is one means of testing the length of life of bees. When they have no queen capable of producing bees to supply the daily loss, it is rarely the case that a colony will survive more than four months except in winter; hives in this condition labor with less assiduity. Some say they will gather no bee bread while they are queenless, as they need none for brood. This is not the case, although they will not gather so freely, and they defend themselves less vigorously against worms and robbers. A queen may die at any time, but the four-fifths of the failures take place just after swarming, when the young queens fly out to meet the drones. That they do this has ceased to be a question among intelligent practical bee men; also, that one impregnation is effective for life. Queens generally fly out for this purpose about noon, or a little after, when they are a week old. Sometimes they are out a few minutes, at others an half hour or more. They sometimes mate with drones at considerable distance from home. When there were no Italian bees in this county, except close to Cadiz, I found a number of hives three or four miles from town that had queens which had been fertilized by Italian drones and produced a mixed progeny. However, when drones are numerous in an apiary, queens seldom have to be out long or fly far to meet them. On their excursions they are liable to be lost from various causes, or on returning, may enter the wrong hive and be lost; as setting hens whose nests are crowded together two hens will get on one nest and leave the eggs of the other to perish. When a colony has lost its queen it will manifest a good deal of excitement, running in an agitated manner about the entrance, and over the front of the hive, especially in the morning; but in two or three days this will generally cease, and I know of no other external sign by which their condition may be certainly ascertained; so that it is well to keep a look out for such signs at the time the young queens would be flying out; that is, in old hives about fifteen days after the first swarm leaves, and the casts about six days after they come off. Of course the time may vary from these rules several days. If a colony has lost its queen at such a time it has no brood and cannot produce another. To supply it run a little swarm into it, if there is no queen on hand for this purpose; or take a queen from another hive and give them, letting the other rear a queen for themselves. Brood might be given to the queenless colony and let it rear its own; but it would be about six weeks before they could have any brood hatching from the queen they would raise. The hive would be too much weakened by this time. Swarms have no brood hatching for twenty-three days after they issue; by this time they will generally be reduced in numbers one-third. If movable comb hives are used they can be opened out, and five or six days after the time the young queens should have been fertilized, and if eggs can be found in the cells, all is right. But if a box hive is used you will have to wait fifteen or twenty days, until the brood will have time to be capped; then invert the hive; smoke the bees down off the combs; press the combs gently apart, until you can see a considerable distance down between them. If there is any brood there it can be seen. One will soon learn to distinguish between brood capped over and honey capped. If queens are lost in swarming-time there will generally be some hives that have given off swarms a week previous, and have young queens not hatched; in such a case get one of the cells and put in the queenless hive. Either put it in the lower end of the combs, so it will not fall out, or insert it in a hole in the top where the bees will gather on it. If she has hatched there will be a hole in the end of the cell through which she has emerged. Sometimes they will have a queen that is not fertile; or if they have been long queenless they may have some fertile workers laying eggs. In such cases they will not have so much brood, and what there is of it will be all drone brood, even in worker cells. It will be known by the ends of the cells protruding much beyond the other cells. In case they have a fertile worker it can be known by inspection in movable comb hives by the eggs being laid very irregularly. Some cells will have no eggs in them; others, a half a dozen to a dozen. In case of the imperfect queen, remove her and give them a perfect one. The loss of queens at swarming-time will likely amount to one in fifteen. The number lost at all other seasons of the year will likely average one in thirty. It is well to give them all an examination in September and again early in the spring, to see if they have brood, and all is right. Young bees thrown down is evidence that they have brood and consequently a queen. If a hive retains its drones long after others have killed theirs, it is a bad sign, for they will not kill their drones if they are queenless. If a good colony is queenless in the fall give them the queen of a late swarm, or run the late swarm into it. The spring is the worst time to remedy the evil. If they can survive until the drones appear, they might be supplied with brood so as to have a queen reared by the time the drones hatch; otherwise, I have found but little advantage from such, except to save what honey and combs they have to put a swarm in.

HIVES.

The innumerable arrangements that have been devised for a home for bees gives expression to a feeling of dissatisfaction with all previous plans. There is an abiding impression that we do not get the good of our bees that they are capable of yielding; that we need a control of them that we have not reached; a vague idea that something can be done with bees that never has been done, and that somehow, this is to be accomplished through a modification of the hive. The attempt to gratify this desire has given rise to a great host of hive vendors, who, I suppose, are in the main honest, or at least as much so as those engaged in other employments, aiming mainly of course at what will take best. Often thinking the peculiarities of their hive embrace just what is wanted to successful culture; but are often like the bee-keepers them-

selves, who in their fertile imaginations think they have discovered the *ne plus ultra* in bee-keeping, but when put in
practice they find won't do—there was something they had
overlooked. No wonder that many have grown out of
patience, both with their own and other people's inventions.
I must say a large amount of the abortive attempts at improvement would have been avoided, had the peddlers and the
bee-keepers generally possessed the reliable information that
can be had from books now published on that subject. Some
growing out of patience say : "I do not want any of your
contrivances—give us a natural bee hive." But what is
a natural bee hive? "One they will go to if left to
themselves—as a hollow tree." In this region where
timber is tall they choose the hollow tops of trees ; in the
West, where the timber is scrubby, they enter the lower end·
In countries where they have no timber they enter boxes,
empty hives or kegs. They have been known to go into the
cupola of a building, the walls of a frame house, or the dried
carcass of a lion. Which of these is the natural bee-hive?
Suppose we give all of our domestic animals their natural shel-
ter from storms, it will evidently possess one essential good
quality—that of always having plenty of fresh air. But I do
not wish to become too natural, lest I should turn my horse
wild in the woods and do my farming by hand and my own
traveling by foot So soon as we begin to manage bees at
all we begin to be artificial.

WHAT ARE SOME OF THE DEVICES FOR HIVES.

In some countries they excavate a hole in the side of a tree.
In Cuba they use inverted sugar-troughs. Hives have been
made dear and cheap ; of straw, wood and earthenware. They
have been made large and small, single and double, tall and
low, oblong, square, triangular, hexagonal and round; in sections on top of each other, or sitting side by side, that bees
could pass from one to another, so that swarms could be made
by lifting a top hive from a lower one, or a side hive from
one joining it; some with inclined bottom boards to clean the
hive; others suspended without bottoms at all; some with
honey boxes of various structures and materials placed on the
side of the hive, on the top or at the bottom, or the side of
the hive removed to take the honey; some are made with

special reference to feeding, or wintering, or robbery, or ventilation, and a vast number with reference to getting rid of the moth. I doubt not that under favorable circumstances bees have done well in every one of them, and premiums and the most glowing recommendations can be had for each of them. But I feel *more* certain that under adverse circumstances bees have done badly in each of them. It is not well to be elated by the eulogies bestowed by the mass of bee-keepers on a hive one may be interested in, nor depressed by their blame. For if the circumstances are good for bees they will do well, and people will like their hives; but if from any cause the bees do not prosper the reputation of the hive is in danger. Yet I am glad to know there are beginning to be many who are capable of rendering a rational judgment of a hive. Having studied the various systems of bee-keeping in this country and in European countries, where it is more of a business than here; and having for many years devoted my time most exclusively to the practical operations of bee-culture; having had something to do with almost every conceivable style of hive, though I do not profess to know near all about bees that may be known, yet I hope that I am better capable of judging of the necessary qualities of a good hive than one whose knowledge is limited to that acquired from the experience of having kept a few hives of bees.

Although I may be personally interested in recommending one hive over another I will aim to suppress all interested feelings while I state what I consider the requisites of a good hive, remembering that it would not at all likely be to my advantage, expecting as I do to make bee-keeping my permanent business, to use myself and recommend to others any hive that is materially defective in any particular. The main object in keeping bees is profits in honey. This can only be best attained by keeping the bees in the most vigorous and prosperous condition; as in keeping other stock we aim at keeping it in the most flourishing condition, and after that take all out of it we can. To keep anything at the lowest point of existence is the poorest kind of economy.

Bees require for their dwelling a dark, dry, warm cavity. It must contain space enough to give the queen capacity for laying all the eggs she is capable of and hold honey enough for winter. Whatever they may make more than this the keeper may have; and whatever bees they can spare over what will make a good strong colony may be given off in swarms to increase the stock. Authors differ a little as to the size of a hive best calculated to produce the most honey and swarms consistently with the highest prosperity of the bees. Some recommend hives containing so few as fifteen hundred cubic inches, while others think about twenty-eight hundred (about one bushel), is the best size. Bees have done well in both these sizes. The Eddie hive, and others, containing seventeen hundred cubic inches, of which there are many in this region, do very well. Small hives are perhaps the most profitable in good seasons, yielding the most swarms and surplus honey, but are most precarious in bad seasons. The hive which I use mainly contains two thousand and sixty-eight cubic inches; everything considered, I think this size as good as any. Such a hive, if full, will contain fifty pounds of honey. Of course it is never full when occupied with bees, as a portion of the combs that would likely contain ten or fifteen pounds of honey will be filled with brood at the time that bees are storing honey. But as not one colony in fifty will consume twenty-five pounds of honey (the average is perhaps under twenty pounds consumed from November to April), there will be considerable surplus in such a hive if it has been reasonably well filled. I have observed a colony that will not fill a small hive will not fill a large one. The only advantage in the large size is, that a surplus of honey may be kept over from year to year to be ready for a season in which they cannot fill their hives. Instead of keeping much more honey in the hive than is yearly needed, I prefer to have a few full frames or surplus boxes on hand, and in case a colony is likely to starve give them a box or frame, or feed them otherwise. This size of hive is used with entire satisfaction by the most extensive bee-keepers two degrees north of here, where the winters are longer; yet if I was compelled to change the size of my hive I would make it larger instead of smaller. In the sized hive I use the bees will generally keep it well filled, which is desirable. It gives room for brood equal to the laying capacity of most of queens, and gives off very respectable sized swarms, and will give them earlier than a larger hive will.

SHAPE OF HIVES.

The shape of a hive is of no great importance. A hive nearly square is perhaps best, as it enables them to keep their

brood more compact, for hovering over and to store their
honey close around it, where it will be most accessible to the
bees in winter without leaving their cluster far. L. L. Langstroth says the most prosperous colony he ever had was in a
hive four inches deep—broad and flat. Some want an inclined bottom board, that the hive may be kept cleaner and
the worms roll out. This would seem like a very simple
means of giving much assistance to the bees; but they are
more bother than profit, as living worms when they fall generally have a chord attached to them and can crawl up again
if they wish, and dead ones do but little harm. Besides, if the
hind part of the stand be elevated an inch or two higher than
the front, the inclination of the bottom will be such that the
constant going out and in will keep the bottom board as clean
of comb cuttings and filth as though it had an inclination of
forty-five degrees. If I do not use a movable comb hive I
want the bottom open that I may invert the hive and examine
through the bottom.

DIVIDING HIVES ARE OBJECTIONABLE.

For if the plan is adopted of setting one hive on top of another, so as to remove one of them to make a swarm, one of
the hives will contain most if not all the brood and most
likely the queen, whilst the other will have no queen and
probably no brood from which to rear one; and even if a
queen was furnished them, the combs would likely be so filled
with honey that there would be no place for eggs. And even
if it were empty, the cells would generally be built for store
combs and could never make a prosperous colony; the same
is true of hives that divide latterly, to make two of one by
dividing it in the centre, and putting an empty half to each
full one. One half will likely contain most of the honey and
the other the most of the brood. But it would be too tedious
to enumerate the advantages and disadvantages of the various
kinds of hives in use. Doubtless very many of them possess
some advantages; but in nineteen cases in twenty their
complexity, cost of getting up, or in some other way, the advantages are overbalanced by the disadvantages. So that I
would recommend the larger portion of bee-keepers to retain
a simple style of hive, which I myself would use did I not
find a necessity of using a hive with movable frames.

4

BEST BOX HIVE.

No difference what kind of wood is used so it is dry and not inclined to warp; inch board is a good thickness. Use two boards fourteen inches square for the sides, the rear board twelve by fourteen, the front twelve by thirteen and three-fourths (this being a fourth inch short at the lower end will make an entrance for the bees). Make the top board fourteen and one-half by fourteen and one-half; make the side boards stand on their ends; bore an inch hole in the middle of the front—it might have a button to cover it when needed. It seems to be an advantage to have combs built nearly straight and of a uniform thickness. This can be secured by using eight triangular strips twelve inches long, the sides each one inch; nail these to the under surface of the lid where the bees are to start the combs; place them at equal distances from each other and parallel with the sides of the hive. These strips are best to be rough as they came from the saw, as bees prefer a rough surface to fasten their combs to; they also like a sharp edge to start from; so that with this arrangement eight combs are almost invariably started from front to rear—each one a suitable thickness for brood when needed to be used for that purpose. Persons who never tried to guide bees in this way to build their combs straight, are apt to say: " Bees will build their combs just as they please;" so they will, and just as the keeper pleases, too, if he understands guiding them: as a horse turned loose in a stable with hay in the rack, it is always quite certain at which end of the stall his head will be. The man who was in the habit of placing candy jars and glass tumblers on top of his hive to be filled with honey, instructing his bees to that effect by writing on the outside of the glass, was always understood best when a small piece of comb as a sample was stuck where he wanted them to commence (bees dislike to commence on glass as it is too cold and smooth). But to return to the hive. It is now all the bees want for their accommodation; but the keeper wants the surplus honey and the swarms—how will he best get them? The brood is reared in the middle or lower part of the main chamber of the hive; the bee-bread is placed around the brood; the honey is placed outside of that in the sides, but mainly in the top of the hive away from the entrance and the light. So, if holes are made in the lid to let bees pass up into the honey receptacles, as soon as the lower chamber is filled they will pass up and store their honey where it is not likely the queen will go to lay her eggs, and consequently no bee-bread be deposited. The boxes in which the surplus honey is deposited are called honey boxes. For convenience the holes in the honey boxes and those in the top of the hive should correspond. It would be desirable to have all kinds of hives and honey boxes throughout the country alike in this respect; so that any honey box would fit on any hive. By purchase and otherwise they are becoming constantly mixed, besides persons often wish to purchase honey boxes when they do not want hives. To supply this demand carpenters could always keep boxes on hand. Perhaps as good a plan as has been devised for taking surplus honey is the following :   .

TO MAKE THE HOLES IN THE TOP OF THE HIVES

Draw four lines on it parallel with the four edges, four inches in; where these lines cross bore holes with an inch or inch and a half bit; if two one-fourth inch strips were cut out from hole to hole across the direction the combs run, the bees could pass up freely from between any two combs and save much labor in hunting the place to pass up.

TO MAKE THE BOXES,

Use 10x12 glass cut through the middle both ways; for the top and bottom use boards one-fourth inch thick by six and one-quarter inches square. Four corner posts five-eighti square and five inches long; drive a brad or small lath nail through the corners of the boards into the ends of the posts; set the posts one-eighth of an inch in from the edges of the boards. You now have a frame ready to receive four lights of 5x6 glass; to hold them in place use triangular pieces of tin, such as are used by glaziers in tacking glass in windows, only make them one and one-fourth inches long and wedge shaped. Split the head end of it one-fourth of an inch; make a hole diagonally through the post from the outer corner about mid-length of it with a pointed blade, to receive the tin which is run through and clinched. When the glass is laid on, one side of the head of the tin can be turned one way and the other the opposite way to hold the

glass. The posts are best made of linn or other soft wood.
If many are to be made the posts should be steamed or put in
hot water to soften them, then holes to receive the tin
punched with a thin punch similar to a shingle punch; bore
a hole in the centre of the bottom; the box turned upside
down shuts the bees down; to get the honey out bend the
tin and take the glass from all sides, this can be done and
the glass replaced with less risk of breaking than in any other
arrangement; four such boxes go to one hive. Honey taken
to a good market in such boxes will sell for several cents per
pound more than in wooden boxes, as it pleases the eye as
well as the taste; such a box is very light, weighing about a
pound, and contains six pounds of honey which suits most of
customers. It will sell thus without deduction for the weight
of the box, as it is a convenient arrangement to keep it in.
You thus get paid the price of the box; however, if the box
is returned it can be paid for. It is thought that bees will
make more honey in larger boxes, and some prefer making
one the size of two of these. This is conveniently done by
cutting the 10x12 glass in too lengthwise for side pieces and
making the top and bottom pieces twelve and one-fourth
inches long. If the honey is altogether for home consumption the boxes could be made the same size of wood, or with
glass in one end. This plan has the disadvantage of not ad-
mitting inspection on all sides to see when they are full.
Honey should be taken as soon as the boxes are full as it becomes darker the longer it stands on. Empty boxes should
be put on immediately to be filled, if the bees are still making honey. To take the honey remove the boxes and carry
them to a cellar or dark room, and leave them bottom up,
and the bees will generally all come out and go to their hive
within a few hours. If the bees will not leave there is reason
to believe that the queen is with them, and she should be
looked for.

Do not take honey at night. Bees seem instinctively to
know that this looks rascally and will resent it with double
the stinging they would in day time.

THE CAP OR COVER

Should be made to fit over the honey boxes to keep them
dark—bees work best in the dark. Make it thirteen inches

square inside and six and a half high, the cover projecting over one-half inch on each side. It would be better if the top of the hive were rabbeted all round one-fourth inch deep and three-fourths on; so that the cap will just fit on it. A large number of the box* hives in use that have no convenient arrangement for taking honey could have holes bored in the top, and this style of cap and honey box added. Strips of white comb stuck where it is designed the bees should start their combs will induce them sometimes to start a little sooner than they otherwise would, and they will build only as many combs as are wanted, and where they are wanted. For this purpose all the white empty combs should be saved. Cut the combs into strips; melt the edges in a warm pan; it is better if the pan contains a little resin and bees-wax melted together; stick the comb to its place before it cools. Three combs in a six-inch box are sufficient. The honey can be taken off sooner if the combs are built regular, than when they have some pieces to fill in the corner after the main combs are built. Combs will be tougher and bear handling better if slightly warmed; cut them with a thin bladed knife warmed. Strips of comb stuck to the top of the hive when a swarm is first put in will be a better guide even than the triangular strips described. The hive just described possesses the advantages of simplicity and cheapness—very essential qualities, as any one who has had much to do in selling hives well know—which will help to compensate for some things left out which might otherwise be desirable. It is convenient for examining the combs by inverting it. The cap and honey boxes can be set off so that it will not take up much room in the cellar or bee house in winter. It can be ornamented somewhat if desired by extending the top of the hive, and the cover of the cap out an inch or more, and put in moulding around under it. A window could be put in the side. Paint would add to the appearance of the hive, and make it last longer, but it is no advantage to the bees; white is the best color, as it will not permit the heat to pass through so readily to melt the edges of the combs loose from the sides of the hive, as a dark color will.

* By a box hive, is meant the simplest form of box for bees, or any arrangement in which the combs are stationary in distinction from movable comb hives.

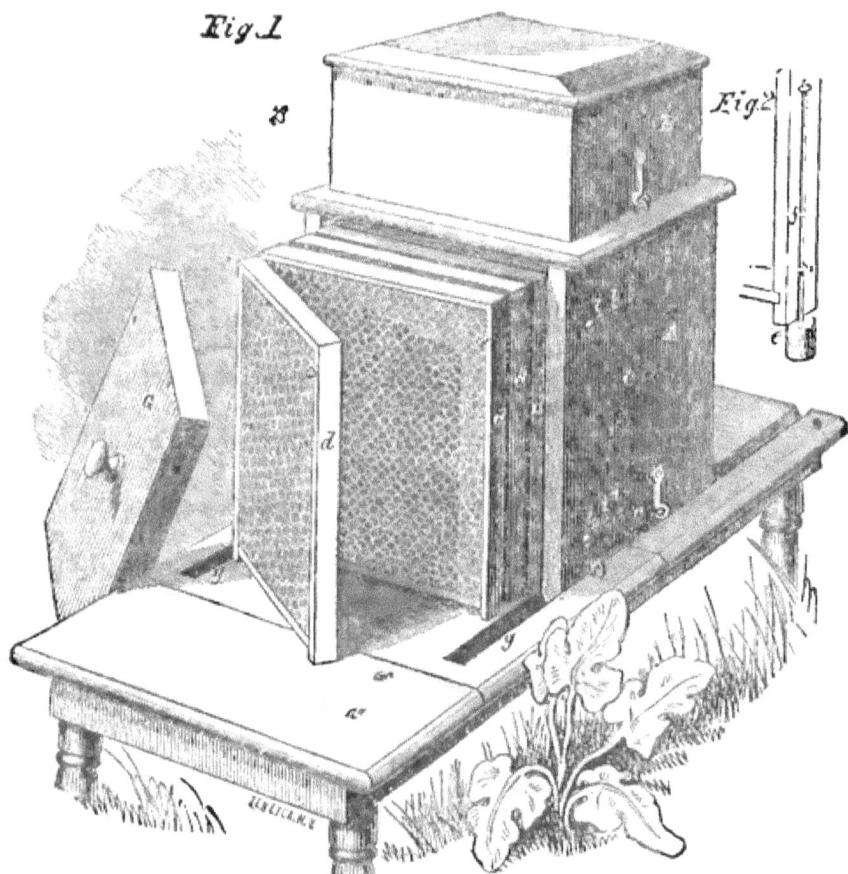

Fig. 1

Fig. 2

THE LEAF BEE-HIVE.

MOVABLE COMB HIVE.

Ten years ago I attended an agricultural fair in Mercer county, Pa., and saw Seth Hogeland exhibiting a colony of bees in a Langstroth movable comb hive. He was lifting the combs and honey with the bees adhering from the hive, and handing them around in the crowd. No one was hurt and no one seemed scared; the bees were composed; no combs were broken or honey running. I viewed the operation with wonder. I there saw something new. Bees I found were no exception to the dominion given to man over the lower order of creation. Bees and bee-keeping were not what I had taken them to be. I purchased "Langstroth on the Honey-Bee," and read with the utmost delight the wonders of this little insect; I concluded I would quit school and go to keeping bees. This seems to have decided my occupation for life. It occurred to me that if bees and their combs could be so handled, there was an opportunity for an indefinite amount of improvement in their management. And so I still view the matter. Although a large number of bee-keepers keep bees just because it is convenient to do so, without making any special effort to get all out of bees that can be had. Yet many who are lovers of nature and keep bees as much to see them do the be-t they are capable of as they do for the profits they yield, will do much to make bee-keeping one of the businesses of the country. Such I believe will always want their bees, in part at least, in movable comb hives, although generally in as simple and cheap style as possible. Soon after commencing keeping bees in the Langstroth and Harbison hives, the Leaf hive was invented and although I considered the hives I had been using excellent, I concluded this, on account of its simplicity, cheapness and ease of working, was everybody's hive. It seemed these would be almost universally wanted if they were known, and as some persons had to work to introduce them and perhaps make some money by so doing, it seemed proper that I might as well engage in it as any one else, and accordingly purchased the patent right of the Leaf hive for two States, and have had the satisfaction of seeing them pretty well tried. Some badly made hives and injudicious transferring in the out-set did the cause injustice, and some extremely bad seasons since have discouraged many ardent bee-keepers. The Leaf hive is just the box hive that has been ascribed with each of the combs made in a frame that can be taken out and put in at pleasure. The frames stand on the bottom board, with stiff wire posts driven in the bottom and running up the side of each frame, to which they are secured in wire loops like a gate on a post. The frames and posts are in no way attached to the body of the hive. One side of the hive instead of being nailed in, is set in loose and is held in its place by nails or wooden pins stuck in gimlet holes. This loose side can be taken away at any time, and the whole hive slid away from the bees. The combs can then be opened away from each other like the leaves of a book, to be examined, and if necessary can be lifted off the hinges and taken out, and if it is desired, empty ones can be put in their place to be filled. They can then all be put in position again and the hive placed over them. If an open space one-fourth or three-eighths of an inch is left between the sides of the hive and the frames, the bees will not generally build any combs in it, but use it as they do the spaces between the combs as a street or passage to go through. In this construction we have the simple box hive with all the combs movable, that they may be taken out and put in at pleasure; and if it is not desirable to do so they can be left untouched, and can be no harm to the bees. It is true that neither this or any other hive will make either honey or bees. But this gives the keeper an admirable opportunity for learning the internal operations of a hive of bees and the condition of any particular stock at any time; and then gives him an opportunity of controlling his bees according to his intelligence. No system of management will be permanently successful, except it be based on intelligence. Neither can a person be said to be a bee master until he can open a hive and handle the bees without dread. The formidableness of this operation disappears after a few judicious trials. It may be expected that the next generation will derive more benefit than the present from this new mode of managing bees, as superstitious notions will be eradicated and the intelligent mode of keeping bees become a habit. Thus, many of the bungling mishaps attending a new mode will be avoided· By the use of this hive it may be ascertained certainly if the hive has lost its queen, and if so, the means of supplying another can easily be given. The presence of worms may be detected, and if found may easily be removed. The combs can be lifted out and honey poured into them to save a starving colony. A comb of honey can be taken from one that can spare it and given to one that needs it. The contents can all be taken out of a hive and put in another while the old one is being repaired. When bees die in a hive they better admit of cleaning the combs to save for a swarm; they are most convenient for cutting out the old combs; they admit of cutting out the drone combs and putting in empty pieces of worker comb to prevent rearing too many drones. When it is desired to get the bees out of any other kind of hive, they admit of transferring both combs and bees to the new hive; they admit of conveniently uniting two very weak stocks; they are very convenient for making artificial swarms. These advantages are not all peculiar to the Leaf hive. There is the King hive, the Flanders hive, the Bood hive, the Lovett hive, the Harbison hive, the Langstroth hive, the Metcalf hive, besides a great many others. It would now be difficult to make any form of movable comb hive without running against some one's patent. Most of these hives are good, but none of them perfect. None of them will be certain always to have their combs straight in the frames without having some empty combs put in for a guide; without this there will likely be one hive in ten or twenty that will have their combs more or less irregular and will have to be cut and straightened. In all of them the frames will be more or less attached to the sides of the hive by combs or propolis. The Leaf hive need not cost more than fifty cents above the box hive; they can be gotten up very cheap if desired.

But bee hives should be made to correspond with the surrounding buildings. Any man who can afford to carry his family in a carriage instead of a spring wagon, or to live in a frame house instead of a log-cabin, can afford to have well gotten up bee hives.

OBSERVATORY HIVE.

"Long from the eye of man and face of day,
Involved in darkness all their customs lay;
Until a sage, well versed in nature's lore,
A genius form'd all nature to explore;
Hives well contriv'd in crystal frames disposed,
And there the busy citizens enclosed."

BEVAN.

An observatory hive is necessary to one who is interested in watching the internal operations of a hive of bees. To make such a hive lift a frame containing honey and brood, and a quart of bees from a full sized hive; if there is no queen with them all the better, as the process of rearing young queens can be seen if there are eggs or young larvæ in the combs. Have a narrow frame made to receive this frame; set a sash containing glass at each side of the comb, so that both sides of the comb will be in full view. The glass should be near half an inch from the comb. Unless the bees be moved a mile or more to prevent them from going back to the old hive, it is best to shut them in two or three days—giving them air; then let them out a little before sundown, so that they will not go far from home that evening, but fly around the hive and mark the place. Such a hive could be set in a parlor with a tube for the bees to pass out and in, under the window.

4*

Tumblers set over holes in the top might be filled with honey. It is better to cover the hive over with cloth for a few days to keep it dark until the bees become accustomed to the place. In such a hive the keeper can at any time show his visitors the queen bee. He can also be sure that she lays the eggs, as he can actually see her depositing them. The process of rearing brood, storing honey and bee-bread, building combs, &c., can all be witnessed.

TRANSFERRING.

Sometimes it is very desirable to get the bees out of a defective hive. They could be driven into an empty hive just before they have commenced gathering honey freely in the spring of the year, and they would do as well at least as a top swarm. But the brood and bee-bread in the hive at that time of the year would be of no value to the the bee keeper, which if given to the colony would be worth as much to them as a medium sized swarm. It is therefore best to transfer to a movable comb hive. To do so invert the hive containing the bees; set an empty box on the top, which is called the forcing box; hammer on the hive to make the bees run up into this box; then set it with the bees on the old stand; pry the side off the hive so as to get the combs out as whole as possible, unless tools made for cutting out combs are used; lay the combs on a table and fit them into the frames of the new hive by laying the frame on the comb and cutting around neatly inside with a knife; be careful to put in all the brood and as much of the bee-bread and straight combs of honey as you can; keep the brood as nearly as possible in the same position in the hive; keep the same end of the combs up; now set the combs all in the new hive and close it up, except the regular entrance; set it on the old stand and run the bees into it as you would a new swarm; then if there is any danger of robbery, make the entrance very small; two narrow pieces of board six inches long should ke kept by each hive to lessen the entrance when necessary; to hold the combs perpendicular in the frames it is generally necessary to set up two or three strips of wood one-fourth of an inch square between each pair of combs extending one-fourth of an inch above and below the frames. I usually put a pair of these strips on each side of the comb and tie them together at the top and

bottom. If the bees are gathering honey they will likely
have the combs well secured to the frames in two or three
days. The hive should then be opened and the sticks or
clamps taken out. Bees can thus be transferred any month
in the year; but it is best, especially for the inexperienced,
to do it as soon as they have commenced making honey.
There is but little honey in the combs at this time, and if
they are transferred out of doors when bees are not collecting
honey there is danger of inducing robbery.

DIFFERENCE IN SUCCESS.

Keeping bees is much like fishing. Two boys get hooks and
lines out of the same lot, procure poles alike, get baits under
the same stone and fish from the same pond—both determined
if there are any fish there they will have them; each thinking
if the other can catch fish, why cannot I. Both become quiet;
presently out flops a big sucker—curving through the air and
down through the branches into the grass. The hook is soon returned, when something immediately seizes and starts off with it.
The self-satisfied youth at the big end of the pole gives it a
whirl and out comes the pumpkin seed or sun-fish. The other
sits half patiently, waiting his turn of luck, but succeeds in
getting nothing but a provoking little nibble, as unsatisfying
as the shake of the hand of the friend who seizes yours with
his thumb and finger. The unsuccessful boy concludes the
fish must all be where his companion is, and seats himself
beside him, and thrusts his hook down by his; but all to little purpose. The other continues to pull out first a silver-
side, next a pike, then a cat-fish—each seeming determined
to swallow his hook and run off with it. He succeeds apparently without effort; whilst his more laborious companion
succeeds in catching only one or two minnows; and after
getting his hook fastened, first in a snag, then on the limb of
a tree, he concludes there is no luck for him that day, and
throws his fish back in the water and goes home, reporting
that he had not been fishing But should the boy even after
two or three such failures conclude that he could never be a
fisher, we would mark him as defective in courage and self-
respect. The elements or the nature of things are not going
to change in order to discommode any one. If any man can
succeed, why not I.

.

[*Extract from the Patent Office Report for* 1863.]

DESCRIPTION OF THE ITALIAN BEE.

The Italian honey-bee differs from our native or black bee in color, size, temperament, productiveness, industry, and power of endurance.

THE QUEEN.

The abdomen of the queen is somewhat more lengthy than that of the native queen. The abdominal rings of the Italian queens do not possess like degrees of brilliancy of color. Whether this is the result of accident, or otherwise, I have as yet been unable definitely to determine, but have noticed that the darker colors (which are few) are more frequently bred in the old dark-colored combs than in new. The bright or standard color of the queens, when first hatched, is of a yellowish or straw color, commencing at the waist and extending nearly to the lower extremity of her abdomen, which is of a dark chestnut brown color, the yellow, as it approaches the three lower abdominal rings gradually blending with the brown, the lower edges of the four uppermost yellow abdominal rings sometimes having a very narrow bordering of darker shade than the balance. When she ceases laying in the fall or winter her abdomen again contracts, its length resembling somewhat its size and shape prior to impregnation.

THE DRONES

vary much more in color. On some, the only perceptible difference between them and the native drone is a slightly lighter shade in the narrow border on the lower edges of their abdominal rings. While the upper half of the abdomen of others will be entirely of a rich yellow or orange color, others are spotted, and a few I have seen, which were almost entirely of a whitish yellow, interspersed with spots of a brownish color. In shape and size they resemble our native drone.

"THE WORKER."

The abdomen of the Italian worker bee is somewhat longer than that of the native. This is more perceptible when it is gorged with honey or returning to its hive heavily laden with honey. The lower extremity of the abdomen is also more slenderly pointed, which, together with its rich coloring, gives it a more graceful and elegant appearance. The three first abdominal rings (including the one joined to the waist) are of a beautiful yellow or straw color. The second and third, and sometimes the first, of these rings or bands are edged with a narrow border of dark brown or black. The first does not always extend entirely across on the back of the bee, and is very slender, each succeeding one slightly increasing in breadth. Queens which breed any workers with a less number of yellow abdominal rings than three, are assuredly not pure. Where they have the full number of yellowish bands, and those bands are of a smoky cast and black, bordering unusually wide, it is, at least, an indication of doubtful purity. It not unfrequently occurs that queens three-fourths pure, breed workers all, or nearly all, thus marked. The temperament of the pure Italian bee is exceedingly gentle. They not only rarely offer to sting, but seldom manifest any anger. Though their hives be opened from day to day the whole season through, the same docility is manifested by pure colonies as when disturbed only a few times during the season, so that this is unquestionably an inherent characteristic. When they do sting, however, it is done with the greatest imaginable determination and force.

There is, however, a great difference in the temperament of different colonies of the impure race, some of the higher Italian grades manifesting much of the gentleness of the pure race. The physical strength and courage of the Italian bee is greater than that of the native, which it speedily overcomes in either single combat or battle array. A colony of native bees, once attacked by an Italian colony of nearly equal numbers, cannot successfully resist them, and soon become its prey, unless timely succor be extended to it. They are by no means conscientious on this point. As soon as they can no longer procure honey from the flowers, they may be found lurking about in search of weak and defenceless colonies, which they soon destroy if permitted. Still, however,

so long as the honey harvest abounds they seem not to think
of robbing.   May we not, therefore, attribute it to their *excessive industry?* for in this they also excel, working both
later in the evening and earlier in the morning, as well as
much later in the season, than the native bee.   Our honey
harvest usually, in this section of country, terminates about
the middle of July.   Last year I found them building combs
and storing surplus honey during a great part of August and
September.   They doubtless obtained it from some source
unfrequented by the native bee, as the latter were at that
time consuming the honey they had previously gathered.
As queens continue to lay in the summer and fall, so long as
their workers continue to obtain supplies of honey from
abroad, they of course breed later in the season than the native bee   This is of vastly great advantage in sections of
country where they are compelled by cold to lie dormant so
great a part of the year.   As they seldom swarm late in the
season, the bees bred at this period enable the colony to enter the winter with a large population of *young* bees, the
larger portion of which survive until one or two numerous
broods have been hatched in the following spring, and the
colony prepared in numbers to swarm, as well as in every
other respect to avail themselves of all the benefits of the
honey harvest the moment it presents itself.   To this fact,
and their great powers of endurance, I attribute much of
their productiveness.   There is, however, one other most
striking feature which, doubtless, is greatly contributive to it.
I allude to the rapidity of their breeding.   As soon as the
weather becomes sufficiently warm in the spring to prevent
the chilling of their more hardy brood, if you will open the
hive and examine their combs you will find entire sheets of
it filled with young in process of maturation, all attended by
a few scattering bees, presenting almost the appearance of a
deserted colony.   This enables them to far outstrip native
colonies of like size in building up a strong population *early
in the season,* which is vital to their prosperity; for, if the
bees are hatched and ready to enter upon their work as soon
as the harvest presents itself, all that can be done may be
and will; but (as is the case, probably, in six-tenths of all
stocks of native bees,) if not hatched until the harvest is one-
half or more passed, of course much is lost; and when we
consider that, in the greater part of the country lying north

of Mason and Dixon's line, the honey harvest lasts only about two months, during portions of which the bees are kept in their hives and their pasturage rendered barren by rains, it will be seen that a few days of *favorable* weather is to them an item of no inconsiderable importance. I have had in a period of two weeks, at the height of the honey harvest, nearly thirty-five pounds of honey stored in surplus honey receptacles, besides building the combs in which they stored it, which, as they consume about twenty pounds of honey in secreting the wax used in constructing one pound of combs, would be equivalent to about seventy pounds of honey gathered by a single colony in two weeks. The great redeeming point in the character of the hybrids is that they possess much of the fertility, industry and productivene-s of the pure race. Their stinging propensities, however, in connection with the fact that they are likely to degenerate rapidly and return to the habits of the natives, will prevent their becoming favorites, aside from other objections which will be found hereinafter.

ITALIANIZING AN APIARY.

This is done by rearing queens from the eggs of the pure Italian queen, removing the native queen from her hive, and substituting the Italian in her place and stead.

REARING QUEENS.

This process is greatly facilitated by the use of the movable comb hive. It is not necessary to employ an entire colony full size; a nucleus of a quart or more of young bees, with three or more combs, will answer tho purpose even better, as the time consumed in examinations is thereby lessened, and a great saving effected. They are better protected, and in some respects more controllable, by being placed in a small hive to suit the size of the nucleus. Bees, so long as possessed of a queen, will not rear another.

All nuclei for rearing queens must be made queenless, and deprived of all combs containing native eggs which have not been laid longer than six days. They should then be furnished with a comb, or piece of comb, containing the eggs of a pure Italian queen, which if not abundant, the comb containing them may be cut into strips three-fourths of an inch in

width by about six inches in length, and this strip inserted
into a frame of comb, the strip resting horizontally upon bearings of half an inch at its ends, with an open space cut out
between these bearings, and under the strip containing the
eggs, an inch in breadth.   The bees will generally so distrib-
ute the queen's cells along the length, and at the lower edge
of the strip of comb containing the eggs, as to admit of their
being separated without much loss.   The comb containing
the eggs should hang between two others containing a suffi-
ciency of honey and pollen to amply supply their wants.
These combs, however, should contain no eggs or grub young
enough to be convertible into queens; otherwise the bees may
select these native or impure eggs or grubs for queens, and
and rear the pure Italian eggs as workers only.   This is the
more important from the fact that they sometimes transfer
eggs and grub from one cell to another, or from a worker to a
queen cell.   They may therefore take an impure egg or
grub, and by placing it in a cell constructed upon the comb
containing the pure Italian eggs, lead the breeder to suppose
it pure; and should it be nearly so, and produce a progeny
not easily distinguisbable from the pure race, it may be the
means of introducing impurity into the apiary, which, failing
soon to discover, may be so extensively disseminated through
it as to require much time, care, labor, and loss to eradicate it.
   The bees will generally construct upon such a strip of
comb from one to ten or twelve queen cells, frequently by
enlarging worker cells, and extending them, thus enlarged,
vertically downward in the space made vacant under the
strip   The queen cells vary in length from three-eighths of
an inch to one and three-eighths inch, and resemble small
teats, much in the shape and form of a small peanut shell.
Each shell contains a single queen, and as soon as the first of
them is batched she proceeds to destroy all the others by
tearing open, or inciting the workers to tear open, their cells,
when she will sting them to death and the workers drag them
out of the hive.   As the first maturing queen may be hatched
on the *ninth* or *tenth* day after the eggs and grub have been
given to the nucleus to rear them from, it becomes necessary, in order to save all but the first batched from destruction, on the *ninth* day, to provide a similar queenless nucleus
or miniature colony for the reception of each of the young
queens, and to cut out all except one of them, distributing

them separately to each nucleus by cutting an aperture in one of its combs, and fitting the queen cell into it. Great care is required in performing this operation in order to prevent the young queen from being injured or destroyed. Some of them will at that time be found to have just changed into its pupæ or chrysalis stage of development, when they are so tender that a slight pressure, jar, or too long exposure to the cool air, may destroy their vitality. Where these queen cells are distributed to colonies which have but recently been deprived of their queens, and still have eggs or grub young enough to be convertible into queens, they not unfrequently destroy the transferred one, even to the third and fourth trial; and in some instances I have had them to continue it when they had no longer any material for young queens left. In such cases they will sometimes receive a hatched or mature queen; but in others they pertinaciously refuse to receive any, but in that case will occasionally rear one or more from eggs which may be furnished them immediately after those which they had have from age ceased to be convertible into queens. In a few instances, however, they will, for a time, refuse to receive or rear all and any queens. When this is the case, it is best to break it up and unite it to another. These obstinate and contrary nuclei are apt to become infested with *"fertile workers,"* which, while they resemble the ordinary worker bee, are capable of laying eggs which produce *drones only*. In rearing queens the workers not unfrequently, after feeding a number of the worker larvæ for two or three days upon the royal jelly (upon which embryo queens are fed as if intending to convert them into queens), suddenly cease to supply a portion of them with it, and thenceforward supply them with such food only as is used in the development of the ordinary worker bee, completing their development as such.

From the period of hatching to that of impregnation, which, in favorable weather, is generally from seven to fourteen days, many young queens are lost, or perish from various causes, a few of which it may be well to enumerate. They may be caught by the bee martin, become exhausted, fall to the ground, become chilled, or, from exhaustion, be unable again to rise, their wings being short; sometimes when she flies out the workers follow her, as in swarming, and all desert their home together; at others they attempt to enter another hive, and are stung to death by its inmates. Occasionally, when all return to their own domicil, the workers, as if displeased with the procedure, seize their queen, and, forming themselves into a knot, squeeze her to death. I am by no means confident that this affectionate embrace springs from maternal affection; still they might sting her to death in a moment, while I have known them to be engaged in this hugging process for three successive days together, and the queen still living, while in other cases they will continue to hug her carcass for several hours after life has become extinct. As soon as they discover her decease they drag her to the entrance and cast her out of the hive.

After impregnation has taken place, and she has safely returned to her hive, losses are comparatively few, unless the nucleus hive or colony be too small to satisfy her prolific demands, when she will disencumber herself of eggs by depositing them on the edges, or in large numbers in the cells, and then desert and seek a wider field for her operations by entering, or attempting to enter, another hive, in which effort she generally perishes. At other times, in such small nucleus hives, the population becomes too dense for comfort, and they "swarm." Usually, however, in such cases, as in starving, it is rather a desertion than swarming, as no queen cells or workers remain behind. When they become too densely populated I divide them, or rob them of brood before hatched, in order to prevent it. Where they chance to become too weak I furnish them brood from other hives; so also with honey, thus keeping them in proper condition for my purposes.

In all cases where the young queens become impregnated by the native or impure Italian drones they should be supplanted by others as speedily as possible, reared from Italian eggs of unquestionable purity; and this precautionary process should be repeated until every colony in the apiary is supplied with a queen of undoubted purity.

INTRODUCING QUEENS.

The worker bees manifest great affection for their queen. I have more than once been stung by them. When catching or holding her she would utter a cry of distress. When deprived of her they manifest the greatest sorrow and anxiety for her recovery, yet, on hastily returning her an hour or more after, I have seen them, in some cases, instantly sting her to death. The cause of this singular and most unnatural treatment was for some time a mystery; but after repeated experiments I became convinced that it was owing greatly to the manner of presentation, and the temper of the recipients when she was presented. Subsequent experiments have confirmed this opinion. The worker bee is exceedingly watchful and impulsive. The slightest quick motion arouses and excites it for an attack, and if, when in this condition, one of its own sister workers alights suddenly near it she is liable to be seized, and I have sometimes seen her stung to death before the mistake was discovered. Once excited to combat, they seem completely abandoned to the destruction of the object of their attack; and although they quickly recognize the scent of a queen, yet, under the impulse of angry excitement, they do not often stop short of her destruction. The knowledge of these facts has led to the adoption of various expedients for the safe introduction of queens. The first, and probably safest, mode which I shall describe is as follows: In the morning of a pleasant day, when the bees are flying freely, take from one of the most populous hives four or five combs containing honey and nearly mature brood. Shake from them, into their own hive, the old or hatched bees, and hang the combs properly into an empty hive, which should then be carefully closed so as to prevent the escape of the Italian queen, which should then be placed in it. After removing the before mentioned populous colony from its stand to another at some distance, place the hive containing the Italian queen on the stand from which the other was removed, and partially open its entrance. The bees which have been out gathering honey, on returning to the accustomed spot, will enter the hive containing the Italian queen. Gorged with honey, exhausted by the fatigue of a long flight, disconcerted by the apparent desertion which has taken place during their absence, and not knowing where to find their original hive, they will at once adopt the new home and queen.

If this operation is performed between the first of May and the middle of June, by filling the empty space left in both hives with empty frames, two colonies may be formed of the one, which is one method of performing what is called "artificial swarming." But if it be done after this period, and where the scarcity of honey pasturage would render it unwise or unsafe to form a new colony, then the native queen should at once be abstracted from her colony, and a few hours later, when the workers have discovered their loss and have become dispirited by their unsuccessful search for her, the hive containing the Italian queen should be placed on a level spot of ground near its future stand, with a swarming cloth tacked to and spread on the ground in front of it. Then, after smoking or alarming the remaining bees contained in the original hive until they are gorged with honey, they should be shaken from their combs on the swarming cloth. As soon as they have entered the hive, now placed on its stand (which they will do in a short time), on their becoming quiet and composed, open the hive and hang into it the remainder of their combs, thus by degrees transferring the entire contents, except the native queen, from one hive to the other.

This process is somewhat tedious, but I have not yet learned of a single instance where it has been unsuccessful, except by the escape of the Italian queen before any of the bees had entered her hive; and this may be prevented by clipping one of her wings. As a colony will never receive a strange queen so long as they possess a fertile one, in all the processes for introducing queens the first act to be performed is the abstraction of the incumbent queen, and the apprisal of the workers of their loss by shaking the bees from several combs into their hives. This usually so alarms them that they proceed at once to gorge themselves with honey, which renders them so docile and tractable that I have, in a great number of cases, introduced Italian queens as soon after as they indicated their consciousness of the loss of their queen, by their moaning noise, by simply taking the Italian queens by their wings, with the thumb and forefinger of my right hand, and *slowly* and *gently* placing them on the top of the combs of the queenless colony among the workers, *still holding her fast, however, until the workers indicate their willingness to receive and treat her kindly*, which they usually do by offering her food, and such other manifestations of favor as they habitually display towards their own queen. This allays all her fears of violence from them, and when released, which may be done, if kindly treated, within a minute after presentation, she will glide down between the combs with perfect composure, which, in turn, allays all suspicion or excitement among the workers, and relieves her from danger. If, however, on presenting ;her sho is attacked by the workers, she should, without delay, be withdrawn (without, however, making such a quick or rapid movement as to excite the bees), and the attacking bees instantly crushed. In the course of a few minutes she may again be presented, sometimes with success; but if not, she should be removed as before, and replaced with her own nucleus, in doing which the same precaution should be used as in presenting her to the new colony, otherwise she may perish by the cruelty of her bees. On the following day, after smoking the queenless colony until all the bees are thoroughly subdued and gorged with honey, the queen may again be presented as before directed. If they shall refuse to receive her, it is safer to let them remain for seven days from the time they were deprived of their queen, by which time it will be found they have constructed a greater or less number of queen cells upon their combs, in which embryo queens are being reared. All these should be removed, or the embryo queens destroyed. On the following day, after again smoking as above described, the queen may be presented as before.

Last year, iu introducing probably sixty queens by this process, only three or four failed of success. It, however, requires some skill, judgment, and experience in handling bees.

Another method is to first remove the incumbent queen, and on the following day prepare a small fine-meshed wire box or case (not of brass or copper), about three inches long by one and one-half inch in diameter, with an aperture at one end large enough for the free passage of the queen. In this cage should be placed a small piece of honey-comb containing enough honey for the queen and half a dozen bees for a period of four or five days. The queen, with half a dozen "workers," should then be placed in it, and the entrance of the aperture closed with a covering of wax, the cage suspended firmly between two combs in that part of the hive where most of the bees are clustered, and in such position that the bees in the hive may communicate readily with the queen, and have free access to the wax-closed aperture. They will soon gnaw it open and release her. Several other contrivances have been resorted to, but with limited success.

I succeeded, in my early experiments, in making some safe
introductions by immersing the queen in honey at the time
of presenting her, but found, ultimately, that unless the recipients were in the proper *mood* at the time of her presentation, they would sometimes kill her.

PROFITS AND IMPORTANCE OF BEE-CULTURE.

The profits of bee-culture, like other pursuits in life, depend greatly upon the knowledge of the subject possessed by
the bee-keeper and the *proper management* of his bees. The
difference in continuance and abundance of pasturage in different localities will of course produce widely different results; but there are very few, if any, localities in the
United States habitable by man in which bees *properly man-
aged* will not pay a bountiful compensation for their cultiva-
tion, while in the more favorable localities four or five hundred per cent. per annum is no unusual product.

According to the census of 1850, there were produced in
the United States and Territories in that year 14,853,790
pounds of beeswax and honey, while that of 1860 is 1,357,-
864 pounds beeswax and 25,028,991 pounds of honey, showing an increase of about 77¾ per cent.

Prior to the publication by Mr. Langstroth of his excellent
work on bee-culture, and the introduction of his movable
comb system of bee-keeping, the pursuit had for some years
been gradually, and in some localities rapidly declining, owing greatly to the ravages of the bee moth; inventions of
hives *for* the prevention of which are not lacking in either
abundance or variety. Many of these, however, instead of
preventing it, proved most excellent auxiliaries for the spread
of its devastations; while others, perhaps from ignorance of
their habits, were so constructed as to prove, sooner or later,
certain destruction to any colonies that might be placed in
them. Several kinds of these hives had been extensively
used throughout a great part of our country, producing destruction wherever introduced, until repeated trials and dis-
appointments had driven bee-keepers generally to the con-
clusion that profitable bee-culture had ceased to be practi-
cable in this country, and so discouraged many as to cause
them to abandon the pursuit entirely. The expectation that
any hive, *of itself*, will ever be found to prevent the ravages

of the bee moth, is an absurdity, which none but the ignorant
or malicious will assert. The *bees* themselves are the only
safe and efficient protectors against the moth, and *where properly cultivated* are *fully competent* to the task. Still, until
the requisite knowledge of the subject becomes generally disseminated, this prejudice will doubtless continue to a greater
or less extent to exist. It is, however, most encouraging to
know that already there are a few extensive apiaries in different sections of our country, which, under enlightened cul-
tivation, produce annually an average of from five to fifty
dollars' worth of honey and wax to each colony; the quantity varying in consequence of difference in locality and management.

[From the American Bee Journal.]

"The results of experience, however, have already been
clearly transmitted to us by the ancients; who, confessedly
deficient as *theorists*, were unquestionably good *practical* api-
arians, and most unequivocally preferred the Italian to the
common bee."

"Count Stosch [of Germany] remarked that the demand
for Italian bees is at present extensive and urgent. It is
easier now to sell ten colonies of these than one of the common kind He who wishes to find a sure market, must cul-
tivate Italian bees, even if it were true that intrinsically they
are of no practical value. He who would sell his wares, must
adapt them to the prevalent taste and the fashion of the day."
—Rev. G. KLEINE.

"I have been quite surprised, in my experience with Italian bees, at their success compared with the common. I
could not credit the report of their great superiority, as in
everything they seemed so like our common bee, except in
the colony. I am now quite ready to believe that their introduction into this country will not only greatly increase the
interest in bee-culture, but they will be the means of greatly
enhancing the profits of the apiary with the same management."—L. P.

"One of the best ways I have found for introducing the
queen, is to make a swarm in the usual way by removing the
parent stock. The bees will receive her in two or three
hours without any difficulty."—C. W. T., HOLMESVILLE,
Chester county, Pa.

INDEX.

LEAF BEE-HIVES.

I keep for sale the Leaf Bee-Hive, made of good pine, the loose side or door framed to receive an 8x10 light of glass, and a shutter to cover it so as to present the appearance of a panel. A set of glass honey-boxes, which retail at 80 cents per set, separate from the hive, go with each hive.

TERMS:

I will dispose of Township and County Rights on very liberal terms, especially at a distance from my own location, as I am determined to sell all except such as I have time to canvass myself.

The price of an individual or family right to make and use the Hive is $5.00.

Hives, $3.50.

Quinby's Mysteries of Bee-Keeping Explained.

Containing nearly 350 pages. One of the most practical works on Bee-Keeping ever published; is replete with valuable information on making either the common box hive, or movable comb hive; the general management of Bees; transferring Bees; making artificial swarms; uniting colonies; feeding; wintering; defending against the bee moth and other enemies of the Bee; loss of queens; how to obtain the most honey in the most marketable manner, etc.

Some such a work I consider essential to the main portion of Bee-Keepers, in order to successful management of Bees, as the want of knowledge on the subject is the principal reason of failure in Apiarian pursuits. A careful perusal of the work will show at once the causes of the various perplexities common to Bee Keepers, and why impostors have palmed so many impositions on the community.

Price by mail, $1.50.   Sold by   R. WILKIN,

Cadiz, Harrison Co., O.

www.ingramcontent.com/pod-product-compliance
Lightning Source LLC
Chambersburg PA
CBHW032357280326
41935CB00008B/612